Judy's World

The Inspiring Triumph Of Our Miracle Girl

Judy's

World

The Inspiring Triumph Of Our Miracle Girl

Nicholas & Eunice Letting

Foreword by Dr. David Mutonyi Muturi

Published by Sahel Publishing Association,
a subsidiary of Sahel Books Inc.
P.O. Box 18007—00100
Nairobi, Kenya
Tel: +011-254-715-596-106
For questions and orders log on to:
www.sahelpublishing.net

A Sahel Book
Nairobi. New Delhi. London. Charleston
Editor: Sam Okello
Interior designed by Hellen Wahonya Okello/Phillip Ojwang
Cover designed by Hellen Wahonya Okello
Printed in USA

To our beloved daughters:
Janet, Dorothy, Joan and Joyce

Foreword

Judy's World: The Inspiring Triumph Of Our Miracle Girl could not have come at a better time, when Judy has finally overcome early threats to her life. When you have a seriously ill child, it can be hard to reconcile that reality with your religious beliefs. Scary diagnoses, endless hospital days, scurrying to specialists and loss of sleep can be challenges that try your faith and make you question faith at a time you need it most. In this book of reflection, Nicholas and Eunice Letting offer a calm voice, a common experience—and a way to view even the most heart-rending events as the work of a loving God.

The inspiring triumph of their miracle girl starts with reflections by the authors about how in every man's life there will come a day that something life-altering happens; a thing so profound and so far-reaching in its implications for self and for others that he stops to take it all in and seek a higher power. The book's a size is great for tucking into a purse and dipping into when needed to fill idle hours of anxiety or in moments of a need for inspiration. Its language is clear so that those with special needs will gain from it as well. For those who share its core beliefs, or are trying to hold onto them, the book is a good source of comfort, peace and perspective.

I had the opportunity to work with Dr. Nicholas Letting at the time Judy was born and when she had to undergo a series of medical procedures in many hospitals in Kenya and Uganda. I wish Judy a very successful future.

Dr. David Mutonyi Muturi,
Chief Executive Officer,
The Kenya Institute of Management

Table of Contents

Prologue

On the day a renowned Kenyan neurosurgeon came to the hospital room where little Judy lay and operated on her head without our knowledge or consent, I finally broke down and pleaded with God to tell me what was going on. Why were things going so wrong and why had He let us endure so much suffering two months ahead of Judy's birth? Our confusion was compounded by the fact that we had four daughters whose births had been normal and so we had looked forward to another joyful delivery; not a heartbreak. After all, hadn't I asked God for daughters before Eunice and I married and He had provided according to His riches in glory? And hadn't I been a wonderful Christian through the years? So what was this about? Why had the past couple of days been such a roller coaster ride when it should have been a celebration?

This painful evening, I took my confusion home and stormed through the mahogany door without my usual knock or exuberance. I scared my sister, Sylvia Lelei, who was staying with us, but I was in no mood for niceties tonight. All I wanted to know was *why?* Why had the doctor done it and why had God allowed it? So I got into the house and walked straight to the bedroom; and even though I have never said it before, I caught a tear rolling down my cheek. The pain of what Eunice and I had been through finally hit hard and I could no longer play superman with the Creator of the universe.

I wanted Him to come down right now and talk to me, give me a shoulder to cry on; tell me that everything would be okay because right now nothing seemed to be working.

The worry of Eunice's recovery from her high blood pressure had now been replaced by the worry of Judy's recovery from a strange illness that made her head swell and hurt and cause her to cry. Her shrill cry all but broke my heart!

In that hour of anguish, I did what Dad and Mom taught me to do when I was a little boy growing up in Mosoriot, in Nandi County. I went down on my knees and asked God to take the heavy burden off our shoulders.

Eunice and I had already endured our fair share, I told Him. I reminded Him of the many promises He had made in the Bible to protect those who called on His name; and even promised Him that Eunice and I would do whatever it took to make things right through repentance if the suffering and pain we had gone through was a product of a hidden sin in our lives. For the sake of our precious Judy, that innocent child, we were willing to do anything, try anything the Lord asked us to!

But as I prayed, I just couldn't take my mind off the events of the afternoon. At around 3:00 p.m., I had gone to see Eunice and Judy at the hospital. This is what I saw…

Eunice's high blood pressure, which had remained abnormally high since two months before her delivery, had stayed high— and this was now a week after delivery. Because of it, she had been on and off at the hospital for the situation to be monitored and kept under control. This afternoon, when I got to the incubator, where Judy was supposed to be, I expected to see Eunice there with the baby because it was her preferred time to be visited, but she wasn't; and neither was the baby. I was shocked. I wondered what could have happened to warrant Judy's transfer from her incubator to another station. Was she okay or had something gone wrong?

In my state of shock and fear, I walked to the receptionist and asked what was going on. "Where have you taken Judy?"

The receptionist looked oddly at me, then she said, "Sir, Judy was operated on; she's recuperating in the Operating Room!"

I was stunned. *Operated on?* "Why wasn't I informed this would happen? Did you tell Eunice?"

She shook her head. "I thought the doctor told you!"

"The doctor didn't tell me anything; and I'm certain he never told Eunice either because she would have told me. So, whose consent did you seek to carry out the operation?"

The receptionist called a nurse, but she was of no help, so I left her fumbling with the phone and went to find the doctor. When we came face to face with the man, I didn't mince words. I was furious. "Why was my daughter operated on without my consent?" I demanded.

By the way he reacted, I could tell my question startled him. You have to keep in mind that he was reputed to be one of the nation's top neurosurgeons, a man who was supposed to be versed in matters of procedure.

I said, "I am wrong to have expected a call and a consent form from you, sir?"

"Look, my brother, I was only trying to save your daughter's life," he said in a hushed tone. "I didn't mean any harm."

"I understand that, Doc, but the question I'm asking is crucial to my perception of you and my continued trust in this hospital. So answer me. Isn't it the right procedure to at least notify and seek the consent of a child's parents before such an operation is carried out? Shouldn't someone have had the courtesy to give us a call?"

"You are right, sir. To be honest, I thought the nurse talked to you about the operation, because I was called to handle this situation nearly three weeks ago. I thought the basics were done. I apologize that something was overlooked."

So there I was. The nurse had just said it was the doctor to tell us; the doctor was now saying it was the nurse to tell us. Why was this happening? Frustrated, I walked to the administrator's office and lodged a complaint. I wanted to help the hospital understand that matters such as my family was dealing with were grave and should be taken seriously. I lodged the complaint then left. I drove home in a state of anger, panic and hopelessness.

When I got home I went into the bedroom to pray. But did you ever know how hidden God's face can be when you want to see it? In that bedroom, where Eunice and I had laughed together in good times and cried together in bad times and strategized together when life's challenges called for it, I wiped tears a couple of times as I prayed. It was a prayer of anguish; a prayer of plea; a prayer of intercession for my family. Finally done, I got off my knees, wiped the lingering tears, then came out of the bedroom. I felt a little better after leaving the matter at the foot of the cross through prayer, but I now realized that whatever problem we were dealing with it was going to be protracted, tenacious and only God could tell how it was going to end.

I forgave the rogue doctor and asked God to forgive me for the anger I had directed at the doctor earlier. Later, when I took a walk in the Donholm neighborhood, I thought a lot about Judy and her mom. I wondered what was going on in Mama's mind. Did she have the same fears I had? Had she cried behind the doors in the bedroom or bathroom when none of us were watching? Had she had her moments with God when she'd bitterly asked her Maker why she'd had to endure so much pain?

As the sun finally bowed yonder and the glow of its tail cut a piercing beam across the Donholm skyline, I finally made a critical decision for Judy. I was going to do whatever it took to get her to recover. The many nights of her swelling head and endless tears had to come to an end. Between God and my friends—and the prayers of those who loved me at church—I was going to fight this strange illness that had afflicted our fifth daughter in a way we had never witnessed anywhere before. I was going to spare no money, no prayer and no advice until

Judy fully recovered and became a child like the rest of her sisters. That was my critical decision!

But no sooner had I made that decision than it was severely tested in a most unlikely manner. Let me tell you what happened. Over the past month or so, I had pleaded with God to reveal to the doctors what was ailing Judy.

I had prayed fervently for a diagnosis and treatment. Little did I know that it would take Anne Ngugi, a mother with a child like Judy, to finally put a name to what was causing Judy's head to swell, what made her cry endlessly and what had caused Eunice's high blood pressure to rise to dangerous levels.

Anne Ngugi, after listening to what I had to say, asked me to meet her in Nairobi West, where she was with friends. Not ready to let time pass, I met Anne and we sat to talk. It was a talk of tears for me because the more I talked, the more I saw Anne's sympathy through her glistening tears. She made me sense that Eunice and I were dealing with a tough situation without uttering a word.

"So tell me straight, Anne," I finally said. "What is the problem with my daughter?"

"The condition," Anne said, "is called hydrocephalous."

The long name made me keep quiet for a while. Had I heard it somewhere?

Did it ring a bell at all? Realizing I had never heard of it, I said, "Anne, what is hydrocephalous? What does it do? And is it treatable?"

Anne said, "Nick, don't ever take your daughter back to the doctor who operated on her; that guy is no good. That doctor operated on my child and nearly killed her. You see, that disease is caused by an imbalance in water drainage out of the head. Ordinarily, the water should drain in equal measure as it washes into the head. When that doesn't happen, swelling occurs and the head can grow extremely big!"

Anne's words filled me with fear and I later walked home a troubled father. How big could the head grow? Was Judy's head going to continue growing big until… I didn't want to think about it.

I got home later that evening with the name of the condition, but not anything more. So when Eunice eventually asked me what Anne Ngugi had said, I looked away as I said, "It's called hydrocephalous!"

"What does it do?" she asked.

I wanted to tell her, but I just couldn't. There was a limit to what even the bravest, most prayerful man could endure. In this moving story of pain, horror and triumph, you are about to be inspired by what prayer and faith can do. You are about to come face to face with the amazing power of friendship and the incomprehensible resilience of a child determined to overcome all adversity. This is the story of Judy Letting. We invite you to come with us into her world so you may cry with her, laugh with her, fight with her and win with her. The only thing we are willing to promise you is that you won't leave Judy's world the same person.

Come with us...

One

Two Months To November

In every man's life, there will come a day that something life-altering happens; a thing so profound and so far-reaching in its implications for self and for others that you stop to take it all in and seek a higher power. It happened to Barack Obama in Boston, the day the Democratic Party gave him the nomination to run for President of the United States. It happened to Nelson Mandela the day President Frederik Willem de Klerk of South Africa released him from twenty seven years of cruel imprisonment and set him and South Africa on a path to freedom. It happened to little-known Wangari Maathai the day she won the Nobel Peace Prize to become Kenya's only Nobel laureate to date. For Eunice and I, that decisive day came in November 2008, when our lastborn daughter, Judy, was born.

To get a sense of what that day meant to us, I have to narrate the amazing journey that had brought us thus far. It started with the high blood pressure Eunice had endured for two months now. It was a situation she had never had to deal with during any pregnancy, so it took us by surprise when the pressure persisted and even threatened to take her down. Afraid that such persistent and mounting high blood pressure may harm the child in the womb, with just two months to be born, we decided to see a doctor. This was urgent because as things stood, Eunice and the child were in danger.

For Eunice, their fear was that her rising pressure could cause her to develop other complications that may prove fatal. For the baby, the fear was that Mama's pressure could hurt her growth and create unexpected complications.

"So, are you okay with seeing a doctor?" I asked Eunice on the day we had tentatively agreed to see a doctor at Meridian Clinic, in Donholm. "Should we go today?"

Eunice agreed. "We have no choice, do we?"

Of course we didn't. The previous night Eunice had gone through a harrowing experience of splitting headaches, restlessness and incessant sweating. She had tossed and turned in bed in a manner I had never seen before.

Toward morning, I warned that the time to see a doctor had come and she had agreed that she needed urgent help. So in the morning, before I left for work at the Kenya Institute of Management (KIM), where I was the Deputy Chief Executive Officer, I went with Eunice to our regular doctor. I wanted her high blood pressure brought under control right away.

But our going to the doctor didn't reveal anything we hadn't already known. The doctor, just like we had already suspected, warned that Eunice's pressure had risen to unprecedented levels. In her medical history, she had never had such high blood pressure and the doctor was afraid that it might hurt the baby if left unattended. Judging that Eunice needed her gynecologist's attention, the seasoned doctor referred Eunice to her gynecologist at the Doctors Plaza, Nairobi Hospital. She advised Eunice to exercise regularly, but avoid strenuous activity. If she could do that, the doctor said, her pressure would stabilize. It was critical that it stabilize ahead of her expected delivery, which was now just two months away.

It was also during that visit that I came to admire the tough lady I fell in love with when I was a Marketing student at the University of Nairobi, pursuing a BCom. degree. I recalled those days because the doctor had called me aside and marveled at how Eunice had been able to walk with such a high pressure levels. Most people who had such pressure, he warned, could not even lift their head off the bed and had to be helped with chores; but Eunice had gotten off the bed, walked, albeit slowly, to the car and made it to the hospital. That was not a small matter. But of course our doctor, even though she had been the family doctor for a while, didn't know Eunice the lioness. She was dealing with a prayer warrior, a tried and tested Nandi woman who nothing would put down before it put down ten other women. She would always be the last woman standing because of her strength of character, her faith in an all-knowing Creator, and her determination to sing her song *Kwetu Pazuri* in the face of adversity.

That tough woman I met in her father's hardware store in Mosoriot, one sunny afternoon, was going to get well, I said to myself. I knew she was going to fight for herself, fight for her unborn child and fight for our four daughters, who she knew needed her to be well and alive.

As we later walked out of our doctor's office, I knew it was just a matter of time before her pressure lowered and the dark, angry cloud hovering menacingly over our heads drifted by. And so we went to the gynecologist and she was mean from the beginning. She said there was nothing wrong with Eunice and that Eunice had no high blood pressure.

On her word, we went home. But as the days rolled, we noted with alarm that the threatening pressure was neither lowering nor Eunice' health showing any signs of improvement. Her lethargy persisted, her headaches lingered and her appetite remained poor. In the face of such lack of improvement, we went back to Meridian Clinic and once again the doctor sent us to the gynecologist at Nairobi Hospital. The hospital ran a clinic, where this gynecologist's office was located. Aware our options were limited, and time of the essence, we went to her and this time she said Eunice had a problem.

That was the beginning of a tumultuous journey!

———

From the moment we got to the gynecologist a second time, I could tell she wasn't terribly thrilled to see us again. I couldn't tell what it was about, but I read a lack of interest in us—and Eunice sensed it too. Since there was no time to pick and choose, though, we went on with consultations. Right there, she told us, after conducting tests, that Eunice's pressure was not safe for her; that she needed to be admitted so the baby's development was monitored for a couple of days.

"And how much will that cost us?" I asked.

With a straight face, the gynecologist said it would cost about five hundred thousand shillings, and that two hundred and fifty thousand would be required as down payment.

I froze. "Two hundred and fifty?"

"That's right. You need to pay it so we may get started!" she said and appeared nonchalant about it.

I couldn't believe it. To begin with, we had already come to the point where our insurance coverage had reached the limit and we had no money on the scale this doctor was talking about.

Why were things proving so complicated? In that moment of trepidation, Eunice later told me, she noticed that I walked out of the doctor's office and started talking to friends about raising the money. Meanwhile, the doctor told her to ask me to get my act together before we could proceed. She told Eunice we could go to Kenyatta Hospital and she'd see Eunice there.

Seeing that we had no options, and willing to give her a chance, we decided to go to Kenyatta Hospital, after all, she was a lady from my community, who I trusted had our back.

But did she, really? Our initial assessment of her wasn't a pleasant one, and since then she hadn't given us a reason to be any more confident of her than when we first met.

"We'll go to Kenyatta Hospital," Eunice said at once, not even giving me a chance to interrogate her change of mind.

"Your mind seems set," I said.

"One, Kenyatta Hospital is relatively cheaper; and two, I feel like we may eventually establish rapport with this doctor."

I considered Eunice's words for a moment, then agreed with her. It was better to get treatment at a place we could afford and where the doctor felt she would better serve us. As much as this was a situation that involved us, her opinion counted for a lot because she was the expert. So when the doctor came back to ask our opinion I told her we would go to Kenyatta Hospital, as she had suggested.

She nodded. "That is a great idea, because you get to work with me from Kenyatta Hospital at an affordable price."

"We appreciate your help," I said.

"Then let's meet at Kenyatta Hospital," she said as she saw us off. "You'll be glad you made this decision."

I nodded absentmindedly as I wondered about her aggressive nonchalance. Had she ever made an effort to make the hospital affordable for all Kenyans? Had she ever done anything to save life without worrying about money? Wasn't she bothered at all that an expectant mother as sick as Eunice was could not be treated because money was a far greater consideration than the life of a child and a distressed mother? I was bothered. I left her office amazed that there were folks in Kenya who had sold their conscience to the shilling. But what would later trouble me even more was the government's lack of effort in building a nation where all citizens could afford treatment in any hospital of choice. Shouldn't excellent healthcare have been any good administration's first and urgent priority nearly fifty years after independence? That's what I thought.

But I'll leave it at that. We left Nairobi Hospital and went to Kenyatta Hospital the next day, the private wing. When we got there, this very doctor acted with speed to stabilize Eunice. Her demeanor and attitude seemed to have changed completely and for the first time Eunice and I breathed a sigh of relief.

So had she really changed? We had to take a *wait and see attitude*, but for now my hope was restored in the future of healthcare in Kenya. In spite of our rough start with this doctor, we felt Kenyatta had to be the hospital where Eunice would get treatment so that she could await delivery without further worries. At least that's what it seemed like, until five days later, when her high blood pressure remained undaunted by the spirited efforts of the doctor and we had to make another spur-of-the-moment decision. Saving Eunice to save our baby suddenly became an emergency and all stops had to be pulled.

Two

Five Days At Kenyatta National Hospital

Nestled deep in the woods of Nairobi's exclusive Upper Hill area is East and Central Africa's largest referral medical center. Named after Kenya's founding President, Jomo Kenyatta, the hospital has handle millions of patients since its inception and was refurbished following its inglorious days due to years of neglect by successive regimes in Kenya. That refurbishing was occasioned by a bomb blast in 1998, when murderous al Qaeda jihadists stormed the United States Embassy, on Haile Selassie Avenue, and killed hundreds of Kenyans and some foreign nationals. The outpouring of global support that followed the unprecedented attack saw the upgrading of systems at the national hospital, beefing up of the lethargic blood bank and an infusion of badly needed drugs into the hospital's emptied chemists. As unfortunate as the merciless attack on Kenya was, it had its unintended benefits, among which was the emergence of a new Kenyatta National Hospital—reborn and made credible.

It was to this remodeled and newly-beefed up hospital that Eunice and I arrived on a misty morning. It was about 9:30 a.m. when we arrived even though the sun had not yet kicked away its blanket and the clouds were just as determined to keep the day dull. When we got to the reception, the first question I asked the lady at the desk was how much money we would have to pay. Having been burnt at Nairobi Hospital, I didn't want to take chances. "May I have an idea of the costs please?" I said with detectable apprehension.

Looking at me oddly, the receptionist said, "Not much!"

"How much?" I pressed.

A nurse walked right up to us, but instead of listening to my concerns, looked at the distress expressed on Eunice's face and hurried to find a wheel chair. Within minutes, she was back and I suddenly found myself in front of the doctor—this time friendlier and calmer. It didn't take long before she decided that Eunice needed to be admitted so that her soaring blood pressure could be contained; because now, like the doctor at the clinic, she feared our child could face harm.

Naturally, I was impressed by this nurse and the care here, because the immediate concern was to get Eunice and the baby out of danger. I felt reassured and a sense that the Lord had led us here started to take root in my heart. Maybe the troubles of the past couple of weeks were about to come to an end and normalcy would soon resume in our life. But things just didn't turn out that way. As if life was one endless conspiracy, our long days and nights were just but beginning.

Eunice was assigned a private room and was taken there with instructions to the nurses that her medications be unfailingly administered on time so that her recovery could proceed in a predictable and quantifiable manner.

When night fell, I decided to go home to our girls because we didn't want them to be alone—and with worries about their mother. That night, I sat with the girls in the living room and talked to them about the illness their mother had endured over the last few weeks. They later prayed with me and made me promise that Mama would be okay.

It was when I went to bed that the real drama began for me. I couldn't sleep. Through the long night, I thought about the day our first born daughter arrived in this world. Janet dropped in like a soldier, a proud Nandi princess who slept through the day and played during the night. She was born healthy and strong and never faced too many illnesses.

"You have the girl you asked God to give you," Eunice told me after Janet's birth. "God gives what you ask for!"

"He indeed does," I said.

"And maybe the next will be a girl too!"

I laughed at that because I had indeed prayed that God would give me only girls. You want to know why? It was because of this man in our village who had a couple of boys and three girls. He brought them up well and took each to school as well as he could. Later in life, the boys got into drinking, fun and forgot about their father. The girls, however, got married to decent men and came back to take care of their parents. Seeing that situation play out, I felt girls would take better care of Eunice and I in old age than boys. That's why I asked God for girls and He was being faithful; here was the first.

Two years later Dorothy was born. Like her firstborn sister, she came into this world without much trouble and has gone on to live a healthy, happy life. Joan was the third to bless our life by her arrival. And finally Joyce was born. She was born chubbier than her other sisters and looked like the one who had the potential to be obese when she grew up. Fortunately for her, she has remained trim and beautiful like the rest of her sisters. Those four girls had been the pride of my life and I always looked forward to being home with them every evening. Tonight, however, they were not as bubbly as usual because they could tell something had gone wrong. The giggles and endless stories that usually softened the atmosphere in the house was not anywhere. Even Daddy had dropped pretenses about Mama's health. Things were bad!

But it was thoughts of Eunice that filled my mind the most. As she lay on that hospital bed, I bounced between fear and hope; bitterness and joy; and sometimes deep frustration. I felt all too human because tonight I couldn't do what Pastor Timothy Guto had asked us to do in times of tribulation—take my burdens to the cross and leave them there. I took the burdens there through prayer, but I left with them and carried them through the night; never letting God help me carry them. I wonder what God thought about me. Did He think I was being disobedient or did He understand that I was just a feeble child of His who was facing anguish?

Knowing Eunice as I did, I knew she was also praying and worrying about the children and their daddy. How were we coping without her at home? Were the girls eating well? How about her workaholic husband? One of the characteristics that drew me to her was her prayerfulness. She believed in God like she had met Him face to face and they had struck a deal. So overwhelming was her faith that many times when I appeared to doubt something we had prayed about she scolded me. I knew she was on her bed praying for her healing and for her children. I also knew that she prayed for me to remain strong and see things through the inner eye of faith. I felt her prayers that night because toward morning, after my weary hours, I suddenly felt peace wash through me. I got off my bed and knelt down to pray with her—me at home, her at the hospital.

I wanted my prayer to join hers as they approached the throne of grace. And I didn't dare pray that *your will be done*, I prayed that *bring Eunice back home to us*. It was a selfish prayer, I know, but it was the best I could do under the circumstances; and I know God understood why I prayed so.

He knew that I couldn't afford to lose the love of my life. We had come such a long way in life with Eunice. Our humble life that began the day I met her in a hardware store had taken many twists and turns. We had been to college, had four beautiful girls and were now members of our Nairobi East Church, in good and regular standing.

Our love had grown through the many trials and tribulations we had faced together; and our faith in God had grown in equal measure as the trials were overcome and victories won on our knees—sometimes through bitter tears. So was this new challenge something to fear? Was it going to prevail where others had failed to bury us? *No,* I said with determination after I had prayed. *We shall overcome this as we did others!*

As the day later broke and the sun began to rise, I got up, dressed and hurried to the hospital. When I got there, I found Eunice without any discernible change. I got worried. Had the drugs administered at night, and our prayers, done nothing for her? How could she still look so lethargic and in pain?

I called a nurse to explain how long it would take for the drugs to begin to act. Unsure what to say, she urged me to talk to the doctor. Later, the doctor came and I indeed talked to her. She said there was nothing to be concerned about; that I should let Eunice's body heal without worry because her pressure had been too high. Not knowing what else to do, I obliged.

"How was your night?" Eunice asked as I approached her bed.

"I didn't sleep. I spent the night a wreck."

"You didn't pray?"

"Of course I did. A lot. How are you feeling?"

Eunice forced a smile, then she said, "How are the girls?"

"They had a good night, and I got them ready for school this morning. I know they are already gone." I drew a shallow breath, then I asked again, "How are you feeling?"

Without hiding anything, Eunice walked me through her night. She had been given drugs, her pressure had been constantly monitored and her pain had been managed through painkillers. But that didn't impress me. It sounded pretty standard, like something I could have done for her at home. I wanted to hear sophisticated words, an intrusive, confounding procedure; a great scientific term that she would struggle to remember and she couldn't pronounce at all. That's the treatment I wanted to hear, because that's what would be an indicator of the seriousness with which this matter was being handled. Talk of painkillers and some drugs sounded like malaria treatment; not treatment of a sharp rise in high blood pressure. What was wrong with this doctor? But I couldn't ask them that, so I later left for work and would come back in the evening to assess her progress. I prayed things would be different.

———

Through the day, as I was at work, friends and relatives called to get updates on Eunice's condition. I told them everything the best I could, but when some of them weren't satisfied with my explanations, they drove to the hospital to pray with her.

So when I came back in the evening, Eunice told me that a lot of friends had come to pray with her, most of them from our church. By their coming, I was delighted to share the burden I was carrying three-way: with God, with friends and with myself. I came to discover that it makes one's burden lighter when a burden of that stressful magnitude is spread out like that. It lightened my load considerably.

Over the next two days, nothing changed at all. Eunice remained in the same state as when she first came. The doctor and nurses were baffled by the aggressive manner her high blood pressure was resisting drugs, but they chose not to act as if anything was out of the ordinary. I suspected that on the third day Eunice too started to sense the despair her doctor and nurses were hiding behind the plastic smiles and polite good mornings. It was on the fourth day that the doctor finally called me aside, after I had come back from work, and told me that it would be a good idea to discharge Eunice.

I was caught off guard. "In her condition? Why?"

She explained her reasons and I eventually agreed with her that a discharge would probably be the better way to go. The point was—Eunice's days were drawing close for delivery and the sustained high blood pressure was bad for the baby.

"But why can't it go down?" I asked with frustration. "Why have you failed to lower it after four days? Could this thing be something other than high blood pressure?"

"No," she said. "It is high blood pressure, but I suspect there is an underlying cause that I've been unable to put my finger on. I would love to do other tests, but I fear I may end up eating into time a more relevant doctor and a better equipped facility could use to diagnose Eunice faster. Let's discharge her. I suggest you talk to a specialized doctor at Nairobi Hospital."

All I could say was: *Great idea, ma'am, but where is the money?*

But I couldn't say it loudly. I told her to do what she felt was in the best interest of the patient, then I left. This night, like the first night of Eunice's admission, I never slept. I kept awake to cry to my Lord, to ask Him all the tough questions.

And again, toward morning, a soft voice spoke quietness into me and asked me a question I would carry throughout the one-year ordeal. The voice said, "Nicholas, why is your heart so troubled? Are you the one who created Eunice?"

God?

I got off my knees in a huff and looked up. In that moment of hope and fear, I said, "Lord, I believe; help thou my unbelief." And so I later went to the hospital to get Eunice out. I found her in a stable condition, but not because she had improved; it was because if I had drawn a graph her condition would have neither risen nor dropped. And matters were not helped by the fact that money was now spent. So not only was I broke, our insurance had also reached its limit. If this was where God brought one to find faith in Him, I had come to that place. There was no place else left for me to go other than lay my head on the shoulder of the one who died for me on the cross. He who knew how bitter the cross felt must have known how bitter this cup was for me and Eunice and the girls. We needed to hide in Him and let Him bear this cross for us!

Three

Back To Nairobi Hospital

Two days after leaving Kenyatta Hospital, we decided to go back to Nairobi Hospital. This hospital, tucked at the lower corner of Nairobi's Upper Hill, is probably one of the most expensive healthcare centers in Eastern Africa. Reputed to have all the great doctors in the region, it is the place of choice for the rich and famous Kenyans to get treatment. Its fabulous wards are graded according to class, ranging from those lower and middle class Kenyans can afford to the ones only the upper middle class and the superrich folks can afford. It is because of the big name, excellent facilities and leading doctors that the hospital is so expensive. Without adequate insurance coverage or vast money, treatment at the hospital is out of reach and most Kenyans never bother going to Nairobi Hospital; it is for the rich, they say.

On this day, however, because of the dire situation we were in, we were back to the costly hospital. There had to be a way God could help us access treatment here; and if not, I needed to mobilize our friends to help us raise whatever amount of money Eunice's treatment would cost. We got to the hospital at around 10:00 a.m. and proceeded to the Emergency Wing, where I was sure Eunice would be attended to faster. There, a nurse did the preliminaries, then led Eunice to a room where she would wait for a doctor.

The doctor, a middle aged Ugandan man, swept into the neat room with the confidence of vast experience and proceeded to examine Eunice. Sensing he was a more sympathetic man than the proud gynecologist who had treated Eunice at Kenyatta Hospital, I opened up—hesitantly at first—and told him about our financial situation. We didn't have the money to handle the charges, I warned and sought his advice.

"Don't worry about that for now, sir," he said, his deep voice filling the room like a man playing God.

"I just don't want to be caught off guard, that's all," I pressed.

The doctor said, "I'll tell you what we can do. We have two options as things stand. One, you could let Eunice be treated here and conduct a fundraising to offset the expenses, or two, you could do what many folks do today."

"Which is…?"

"Find a relatively cheaper hospital to take Eunice to and I will be her primary doctor wherever she goes. The beauty of this arrangement is: she gets my services at an affordable price. This is because other hospitals don't charge as exorbitant rates as this one does. The choice is yours."

I suddenly felt hopeful, but I wasn't sure which hospital to settle on, so again I asked him to help us decide where he would be most comfortable.

"Nairobi West? Nairobi Women's? Mater?"

"Mater," I said.

He looked me in the eye and said, "Then get out of here before you incur more expenses than you can handle. I will meet you at Mater this afternoon."

That was a big relief. I asked the nurse to let us leave and she didn't object, especially because the doctor had asked her to let us go. Within hours of our release, we got to Mater Hospital and told the good folks there that we had been referred. It didn't take long before she was admitted and settled in a comfortable room, where the kind doctor would see her later. Her discussion with Pauline Ngelo, on the day we left Kenyatta Hospital in despair, had helped indeed; after all, this hospital was reputed to be among the best in Nairobi and could only be third after Nairobi Hospital and Aga Khan.

At around twelve o'clock, the doctor came to Mater to see Eunice and his other patients. I was delighted to see how methodical he was and even decided to go to my office for an hour or two. It was while I was a way that a sudden and critical decision was made to start the unborn baby on a drug that would strengthen its liver because Eunice could no longer carry the pregnancy to term. It was too dangerous for her and the baby to be under such relentless high blood pressure. Later, when I came back to see Eunice she didn't want me to leave her at the hospital. I had to devise a way of escape by pretending I was going to the toilet. I left her in the hands of the nurses, because hospital regulations did not allow anyone, not even her husband, to be with patients. That night, for the first time, I slept like a little baby. It was because I suddenly felt like the Lord had come down to help us deal with the situation. So was this the end of our troubles?

———

It turned out the reason I had slept so soundly last night was because of sheer exhaustion. I was flummoxed. Waking up this morning brought back memories of the last couple of days and I felt a sudden fear sweep through me. I could tell we were not off the hook yet because the doctor, even though he seemed so confident about the situation, had warned that the baby needed to be separated from the mother—or had I heard my own things? Reflecting on what his words had meant, I felt a need to rush to the hospital, so I prepared the girls for school, then left for Mater Hospital, where Eunice was waiting for me with the news of the child's liver being strengthened.

As she narrated events of last evening, and how the doctor had stressed the need for swiftness, it occurred to me that we were about to escalate to another level of treatment; the kind of escalation I had been looking for.

What bothered me, though, was the word *separate*. Did the doctor mean a procedure where the child was forcefully evicted from the womb of its mother or a more friendly procedure where it was gently nudged to leave its home of seven months earlier than planned?

I decided to ask a nurse. I said, "Help me understand this terminology. Does *separate* mean forced birth? Will the baby be okay if it was forced out of the womb so early?"

The nurse nodded. "It's C-section, and of course the baby will be okay. It's for the good of the baby and its mother."

I felt relief. "When will it be done?"

"Only the doctor can say for sure; I don't know," she said. "It may be today or tomorrow."

Eunice and I talked briefly about the situation, then I left for work. In the time I was gone, many friends called to ask about her condition, and many others drove to the hospital to pray with her. And back at church, people prayed for her every Sabbath, making her a permanent feature of prayer in the church bulletin. It encouraged the girls and I to see that our pastor, brothers and sisters in Christ, and relatives cared about what happened to us. We were not alone!

Later, encouraged by the first sign that a doctor was finally contemplating something dramatic, I went to the office and updated colleagues on the goings-on. I told them about the sudden discharge from Kenyatta, the new doctor we'd met at Nairobi Hospital and Eunice's new home at Mater.

Though the new developments seemed overwhelming to me and to them, my positive attitude made them believe things would finally be okay. I told them that the sad story I had told them for more than two months was about to turn into a happy story with a happy ending.

So it came as a big shocker when I received an urgent call at around two o'clock from Mater Hospital. I was needed there right away and whatever it was couldn't wait!

Four

Judy Is Born

The Mater Misericodie Hospital is located in the middle class residential neighborhood of South B, just off Dunga Road. Considered one of the best yet affordable hospitals in the city, it has served the residents of Nairobi well and has pulled in patients from as further afield as Uganda and Tanzania. But before it became what it is today, the hospital has come a long way. Here is a brief history. The hospital was opened in 1962 by the Sisters of Mercy, a Catholic Order of Nuns originating from Ireland, three years after registering themselves as the Registered Trustees of an entity under the Perpetual Succession Act (the succeeding legislation after independence).

The Sisters of Mercy first set up a 60-bed general hospital to cater mainly for the poor, indigenous Kenyans, with the primary mission being general healthcare. The colonial authorities granted 12 acres of land in a swampy, mosquito-infested area, which has since become the Industrial Area of Nairobi. In 1970, a 60-bed maternity ward was opened with antenatal, postnatal and immunization clinics attached in order to upgrade the quality of maternity healthcare available to the poorer segments of the Nairobi population.

In 1972, in recognition of the contribution of the hospital in training midwives to assist births in rural areas, Mater was chartered as a School of Midwifery. In 1975, a consultants' block of 6 offices was opened enabling specialized consultants to practice on site and deliver significantly better medical skills to the patients. In 1986, the hospital opened its own pharmacy, physiotherapy and laboratory services and, in 1990, opened its counseling center for inpatients, outpatients and staff who need advice and guidance on family planning, HIV, and other concerns of a psychological and/or physical nature.

I have no desire to beat the drum for this great healthcare facility, but I believe it is critical to understand where Mater has come from as we narrate the story of the baby about to be born in it. So let's get back to our story now.

At about 12:00 p.m., the doctor arrived at this hospital and proceeded to the room Eunice was in. His mind was made up about the need for a preterm delivery of our baby because he feared for the life of the mother and the baby.

When he arrived, he immediately gave instructions that Eunice be prepared for a C-section in the afternoon. He wanted her wheeled into the Operating Room by 2:30 p.m. at the latest. Within minutes of those instructions, he swept into Eunice's room and told her what the day held in store for us. "Your baby will be born today," he said.

"Have you told my husband?" Eunice asked.

"Not yet!" he said.

"You have to tell him!"

That's when the nurse called me. I was at work already and wanted to clear my desk of pending assignments, but this sounded too urgent; so I immediately called Elder Enosh Bolo and told him that I had been summoned to the hospital.

In spite of his busy schedule at the Kenya Institute of Management, where he was also a colleague, the elder hurried to my office and we went together to Mater. My reasoning was this—if the news turned out to be grim, on the scale of my wife's death, I didn't want to bear such a heavy burden alone.

I needed a brother, a dear friend; someone I could lean on as my tears flowed and I started to figure out who to call first and what steps to take later. I wanted a human shield!

When Elder Bolo and I arrived at the hospital, we went straight to Eunice's room. She wasn't there. Stunned, I hurried to the receptionist and asked what was going on.

The lady said, "She has been taken to the Operating Room."

"But why? What has happened?" I asked.

"That baby has to be delivered today!"

It was like a thunderbolt. The baby was about to be delivered? Was that the way God had chosen to end our agony of the last couple of days? If it was, I wasn't going to complain; because it was about time we had some relief.

"So what do we do now, just wait here?" I asked the lady. "Or can we see Eunice before the procedure starts?"

The receptionist called a nurse and the nurse went in to consult with the doctor. When she came out, she said we could see her for a minute, just long enough for her to know we were here. We went in and Eunice seemed relieved that I had come.

I told her I would be waiting outside till everything was clear. While we waited, Elder Bolo and I talked about the prayers of friends and the amazing support my family had received. We glorified God for drawing us into a church that molded and nurtured a sense of family. Later, I told the elder about my father. The man, having been a police officer in the paramilitary unit known as the General Service Unit, was stoic and not so sentimental. Officer Joshua Lelei was supportive in his own way, but had never, at any time, talked to Eunice with the splitting voice of a father-in-law worried about his son's wife; or to me as a father worried about his son's son. Having fought in the Shifta Wars of the Northern Frontier District in the late sixties and early seventies, his was dispassionate love, if ever there was something like that.

In our home, not too far from Mosoriot Teachers College, in Nandi County, the old man kept many cows, sheep and goats. He curved the home into a section for houses, which included his; a section for his son's houses, and a vast lawn, where trees and other plants grew. Outside the main gate, he set up a spot reserved for planting grains and certain fruits that could survive the tropical weather prevalent in that part of the world. Like every elderly man in the village, he had a spot where he sat in the evenings and talked to folks in the home about his exploits at work, the way things used to be and how far our community had come. He was particularly fond of the glory days of President Daniel arap Moi and talked in glowing terms about his achievements in the education sector. To him, Kabarak University, Sacho High School, Moi High School-Kabarak, Moi Eductaional Center, in Nairobi, and a string of schools across the nation would have never been established were it not for President Moi.

Then there was the Nyayo Milk program. My father recalled the days of that milk with fondness, describing the act of giving children milk as one of honor. Only a man with a great heart, he said, could see the need to give children milk. The man was not just a President, but a father; that's why the Lord has blessed him with a long, productive life.

"How about Eunice's father?" Elder Bolo asked.

I told him that Eunice's father is a deeply spiritual man who has brought up his children with the love of Christ and solid morals.

When I started dating Eunice, it became important for me to talk to her neighbors secretly about her family because neighbors know things. On the afternoon I finally executed that plan, I sneaked into her neighbor's home and asked about her father, her mother, her siblings—and a lot about her. The neighbor told me that Eunice came from a home of committed Christians. "You won't find a better family in this village than that one," she said.

Elder Bolo laughed. "Are you saying the lady thought of your father-in-law's family as better than hers too?"

"Honest. That's what she was!"

"So you married Eunice because you felt her family was morally upright? Did you date her?"

I didn't know what dating meant, so I was about to fumble an answer, but I was saved by the nurse, who walked down the hall and gave me one good news and one bad news.

"Give me the bad first," I said.

The nurse took time to explain the way things had turned out. It had taken the doctor about thirty minutes to complete the delivery procedure, then he spent another thirty minutes...

"Doing what?" I cut in.

"Trying to stabilize the patient's pressure."

I was lost. Did that mean the pressure was still going to be a factor? Or was the nurse saying Eunice never made it?

"Sir," she said, "your daughter has been born, but your wife is unconscious. It would be better if I let the doctor explain what has happened and what you should expect in the coming days. Come with me!"

Elder Bolo and I followed the agile nurse to the room, where Eunice lay. I could see that she was not conscious, but she wasn't completely unconscious. Looking at her, even that small sign encouraged me. I looked at the bed to see the baby, but it wasn't there; clearly it had been moved.

The doctor said, "Sir, I'm sure the nurse has already told you about your baby girl. We've had to incubate her and she'll remain in that incubator for a while."

"How long?" I asked.

"I can't' say for sure, but it will be more than a month."

I was stunned. *Another month of worry?* But I had no choice, so I asked what else to expect.

The doctor said, "The immediate worry is your wife's high blood pressure. I had hoped it would lower within moments of delivery, but that has not happened. I have also observed that she has an enlarged heart, which may be partly responsible for her unconsciousness. My overall assessment is that she should be treated for high blood pressure until it has stabilized, and we will continue to monitor the enlarged heart."

"Thank you," I told the doctor. As he left the room, I felt as though whatever we had to deal with now, it probably paled in comparison to what we had been through already. With the baby out, it wouldn't take long before Eunice stabilized and came home to her daughters. With Elder Bolo's help, I kept my spirits high and remained hopeful about the future. The Lord was in control!

———

An incubator is a piece of equipment in a hospital which new babies are placed in when they are born weak or born too early in order to help them survive. When I was finally brought in to see our little angel, she was in that piece of equipment oblivious to what was going on. The date was November 28, 2008. Earlier in the year Kenya had gone through one of its worst political meltdowns and the country was just beginning to pick up the pieces. I looked at the little girl shielded within the secure walls of the incubator and wondered what the future held for her. Would she grow up in a more democratic, stable society or would she one day have to endure another meltdown occasioned by bad politics?

Elder Bolo prayed for the child, then we left the corner where she was. Making our way back to Eunice, I wondered about life. Was it true, as Pastor Rick Warren had written in his bestseller *The Purpose Driven Life*, that each of us is born with a purpose? Was it true that the greatest day of a person's life is the day he or she was born and the day he or she discovered why? If that was the case, was my little girl starting life two months earlier than the rest of her age mates still playing in the womb because she had had a head start?

"We have to leave now," I told Eunice.

Feebly, she turned and spoke more with her eyes than her lips. She said, *You can't leave me here alone!* I'm sure she wanted me to linger in the hospital and be sure our baby was well taken care of. She also wanted to tell me about her experiences, but she couldn't talk, which made her feel terrible.

Aware we had to leave, though, because of the hospital's strict regulations, we devised a way to leave. What I did yesterday we would do again today.

So I told Elder Bolo to watch over her as I went to the bathroom, then he would follow. We did that and left. As I later approached home, I started wondering what I would tell the girls about their mother and their new sister. Would I say she was born, but was in an incubator? Or would I say their mother was still gravely ill even after delivery? And just when would Mama and the new baby come home? But when I got home it was like the Lord had cleared a path for me; because right there in my prayer, I told my girls what was going on and they said a big amen when I was done. The only question Joan asked later was: Dad, can I see the baby?

*

Today I look back on November 28th 2008 and see it as the most critical date in our family. On that date, the day Judy was born, the Lord settled among us a daughter who would touch our lives and those of others in some of the most profound ways ever imagined. We went from being a family of six healthy folks to a family that would forever be defined by how we took care of the seventh member, who was born with challenges of a nature we had never dealt with before.

Judy's long walk to normalcy started four days after she was born. It was on that forth day that Eunice and I noticed her enlarging head. At first we thought it was normal and would clear, but when we eventually realized that it was not reducing, we started to worry. It was evident something had to be wrong and the doctor need to act fast to save Judy. If her head was not brought under control, our little girl was going to… no, I didn't know what would happen to her; and that's what scared me more than anything else. Not knowing!

Five

Judy's Enlarging Head

On the fourth day of Judy's birth I understood what David, the son of Jesse, meant when he said: The Lord is my shepherd I shall not want, He makes me to lie down in green pastures... Even though I walk through the valley of the shadow of death I will fear no evil, for thou art with me. Your rod and your stuff, they comfort me. You anoint my head with oil, my cup overflows. Surely goodness and mercy shall follow me all the days of my life and I shall dwell in the house of the Lord forever!

David was facing a situation just like Eunice and I had faced over the last couple of days. Things were not working and there was real fear in the man the Lord Himself had called a man after His own heart. I don't think there is another biblical character that such unreserved accolades have ever been heaped on by the Lord other than David.

But I know that there was Job before him. Job was known to be a righteous man who lived in Israel and was a friend of God. Jewish legend has it that one day Satan went to heaven and challenged God to a duel over Job.

Satan said, "I was down there and I met a certain rich man called Job. Look, that man isn't what you think he is; he only worships you because of the enormous wealth you have given him. If you took away that wealth he will walk away from you in a huff. Do you want to try his faith?"

God said he had no problem trying Job, after all He knew Job's heart. "Go try your luck," He told Satan.

Satan left heaven with a great plan. He arrived in Israel with the fury of ten bulls. From the time he met Job, he unleashed terror on a scale the man of God had never witnessed before. Job was hit with one plague after another and his wealth was plundered in a massive storm that targeted only his homestead.

But alas, Job never betrayed his faith in God. Instead of whine, he said, "The Lord giveth and the Lord taketh away; glory be to his name." Satan went back to God. "Maybe it wasn't Job's wealth; it has to be his good health. Allow me to touch that!"

"You may try your luck again," the Lord said, but He also plugged in a warning. "Do not touch his life!"

Satan left for Israel again. He tormented Job in ways Israel had never seen before, prompting Job's wife and friends to tell him to curse God and die. But Job knew God better than they did.

He told them to cut their losses and leave him alone. Later, Job's great wealth was restored and his good health given back, while his wife and friends were hit with calamities.

In telling this story, I'm not comparing myself to David or to Job; those were men far greater than I'll ever be. What I want to underscore is that even men of valor and deep faith like David and Job faced moments of great tribulation; a time they sought God's face but it was hidden from them. So knowing that David and Job had faced suffering, I felt prepared to face whatever Judy's enlarging head portended; because by now it was clear that we were dealing with a condition of significant distress to the child—and to us as well.

Worried, therefore, that Judy's tender head would distend in circumference and reach dangerous proportions, I asked the nurses and the doctor what the problem could be. Why was Judy's head expanding at a rate faster than her age vouched for? Was this condition fatal? But the doctor didn't say anything other than to suggest we call a neurosurgeon. Looking back now, it is clear to me that the doctor and those nurses knew what Judy was going through, but they didn't want to tell us, preferring instead that a neurosurgeon be the one to break the hard news. I have no quarrel with that, but what I still can't understand is why the name of the condition could not be divulged to us. Why it had to take a meeting with Anne Ngugi for us to finally know what the condition was called. But I'm getting ahead of myself. Let me back up a little.

On the sixth day of Judy's delivery, the doctor placed an urgent call to a neurosurgeon and warned the man to come in at once. The fear was that the drugs Judy was taking were causing her head to enlarge even faster than earlier witnessed. Meanwhile, Eunice was now discharged because her pressure had stabilized and her heart situation had corrected itself.

Like Job, even though Eunice's discharge was a modest development, I felt as if the path to restoration had begun. The dark cloud that still lingered, because of Judy's unresolved condition, would clear in a matter of days. Even so, her retention in the incubator meant we had to visit the hospital every day to see her. We watched with satisfaction as her weight went from 1.6 kilograms, at birth, to normalcy. But we also watched with trepidation as her gain in bodyweight doubled the size of her head. It was so distressing to see her suffer!

A couple of days into this ordeal, the neurosurgeon came to the hospital and, without informing us, went ahead to perform surgery on Judy's head.

He inserted a shunt in Judy's head and lowered it to her stomach to relive the pressure that was steadily building in the head, causing her tender skull to swell disproportionately. That cloudy evening, when we came to the hospital for our regular Judy visit, we were surprised to see the shunt on the girl's head. When we asked what had happened, a nurse explained that the neurosurgeon had already come and operated on the child.

"But we were not consulted," I protested. "Who signed her consent form since her mom and I didn't?"

The nurse said, "I'm so sorry, sir. I thought the doctor told you and prepared you for the procedure. He was supposed to have told you; that's how things are done."

I didn't like that. I left the nurse and went to the neurosurgeon. When I met him in the hallway, he was surprised that I was complaining. "I had to save your child," he said. "Can't you at least thank me for that?"

I couldn't. What he had done was not procedural. So burning with fury, I made my way to the office of the administrator to report the incident. I left that office only after I was promised a thorough investigation and reprimand for the neurosurgeon. Over the next few days, we continued coming to the hospital to see Judy, until the 3rd of January 2009, when she was eventually discharged and we brought her home. And since our insurance had now run out, we were told not to come back to the hospital, since we could no longer pay!

I look back at that incident with fear and trepidation. Can someone tell me what happens to poor Kenyans when they get sick? Could it be possible that there are many Kenyans who die needless deaths because they have no insurance or lack someone to pay the hefty sums hospitals levy on the sick? If that is indeed happening, what does it say about our government and healthcare institutions?

I'll leave it at that.

When we brought Judy home, we faced one of the most difficult situations a parent could ever face. The girl, from the time she came home, cried nonstop. She cried twenty four hours a day, then cried some more! Troubled by her crying, we asked the hospital people what the problem was. They told us she was still uncomfortable with the shunt in her head; she would soon adjust to it and all will be well. As this happened, I had to be at work every day, which meant it was Eunice who bore the brunt of the child's discomfort. My colleagues, aware of what was going on at home with Judy, offered words of encouragement and even asked me to go home on many occasions to help Eunice with the baby. They were so kind and so understanding that I look back today and wonder how much harder it would have been were it not for their support.

Over the next one month, Judy's head continued to enlarge and her tears continued to flow unabated until we decided to take the child to Nairobi Hospital. There, a doctor who assessed her condition said the shunt was inserted wrongly and it was what was causing discomfort.

"So what do we do?" I asked the doctor.

"We have to do another surgery!"

I don't want to tell you how sad Eunice and I felt that day. It was the day we came to terms with the fact that Judy's condition wasn't something that would end anytime soon. So as we got back home, I told Eunice about David and Job. Those two men of God, I said, had endured a lot of pain yet they remained faithful to their Creator. We would also overcome, I said.

"I know we will!"

"But why us, Mama?" I asked her. "Why has the Lord allowed something like this to happen to us?"

Eunice managed a weak smile, then she said, "Sweetheart, if I had answers to questions like that, I would be God!"

Later, as Eunice and Judy slept, I remained awake to have a chat with God. We talked till dawn and the Lord was kind enough to put up with my questions, complaints and lack of understanding. He reminded me that He was God and I was man. When I eventually went to the office, I felt exhausted and my eyes looked droopy. This was fatherhood like I never knew it could be. What was God saying? How come it wasn't clear even though I had prayed so long?

———

"The corrective surgery Judy's doctor told you about is in three days, sir," a nurse called to inform us. "Make sure you bring her in or you may not have another chance for days!"

I couldn't believe it. "Three days?"

"It's the only available day, sir. If you don't come, it may be several days before we can reschedule an appointment; so make sure you come!"

Even though I didn't like the idea of such a short notice, I couldn't do anything to change it, so I told Eunice we had no choice even though I didn't know where the money would come from. I was going to trust God to avail the money; after all, hadn't He reminded me several times that He was the one who had created Judy?

I was going to take Judy to Nairobi Hospital for that operation. That's what the Creator of the girl wanted a weary, beaten father to do!

*

That cold evening, I called Eunice's dad and asked him to pray for us. I also called the pastor and some elders and informed them of our situation. I later went to bed with a light load on my shoulders because I knew brothers and sisters were united in prayer for Judy, Eunice and the rest of our family. I knew it was only a matter of time before the Lord looked down with favor upon the army that had joined the fight to pray and Judy's head would stop getting any larger.

Six

Judy's Corrective Surgery

The story of Abraham, as it's narrated in the book of Genesis, is perhaps one of the Bible's greatest testimonies of faith. The great patriarch was asked by God to prepare for a sacrifice and bring his son along on a trip to the place of sacrifice. He did as the Lord directed, but never told the son that he was that sacrifice; that it was him whose blood would spill. When the son asked where the sacrificial animal was, the old man said the Lord would provide.

Once on location, Abraham prepared the altar, got his sword ready and lifted it in an amazing display of faith in his Creator. But just before he could strike Isaac with the sharp ancient sword, the Lord told him to stop.

And suddenly there was a ram by the bush. "Take that one," the Lord said. It was a test of Abraham's faith.

On the third morning, the day Judy was to be operated on a second time, I woke up early and prayed with Eunice. We were wary of this new operation, but we had to do whatever it took to heal Judy. After we prayed, I asked Eunice if she still had her faith in God. "Do you trust Him to heal our Judy?"

"He is all we've got," Eunice said. Then she asked, "Why are you asking me that? Are you afraid?"

"Shocked!"

"But why? By what?"

I told Eunice about my night. I had not slept much, most of the time reflecting on the journey we had been through. I narrated how it all started, how she had merely complained about migraines, then lost her appetite, then became lethargic and finally we were told she had high blood pressure. That pressure, in an effort to treat it, had brought us nights of pain and moments of prayer with tears.

Then today, as we were preparing to take Judy to Nairobi Hospital for the first time, our insurance coverage was spent.

"Is God testing our faith in Him?" I asked Eunice without telling her about my reflections on Abraham last night. "Is He trying to determine whether we love Him or not?"

Eunice looked at me with a frown, but never answered my question. Had she answered, I would have told her about many other biblical characters who had faced severe pain while serving God. There was Abraham and his inability to have a child; Moses and his leadership of stubborn Israelites; Job and the crippling blows to his wealth and health; the apostle Paul with his burden to correct corrupting theology in a nascent church; Peter with his battle to see the kingdom of God through the eyes of faith and humility; and even Jesus Christ, who in a moment of anguish pleaded with God to let the bitter cup of sorrow pass from Him!

As I thought about those heroes of faith and their struggles, it was the first time the Lord revealed something significant to me. He said: Nick, my son, have you failed to see what this has been about all this time? Judy's condition fits in with the overriding theme of struggle that has played out between Satan and I for years. It is called the Great Controversy.

As long as man is in this world, man will suffer. But take heart, I have overcome the world. Keep Judy safe and keep her happy!

The voice was so distinct that I turned around to look at the place it emanated from.

"What is it?" Eunice asked.

"I'm ready for the battle!"

"The battle? You call going to the hospital a battle?"

I didn't explain what I meant; instead I asked that we leave. We went to Nairobi Hospital and brought Judy to her new doctor. The doctor took a look at the shunt that was inserted into Judy's head and he shook his head in disbelief.

"What doctor did this?" he asked.

I didn't tell him.

Later, as Eunice and I waited in the lobby, we were filled with wonder about our next cause of action. Then, as we were about to leave, a colleague at the Kenya Institute of Management saw us with Judy and stopped us. She was of medium height and was slender; but in spite of it, she was jovial and spoke with a smile and unhidden compassion toward us. As colleagues at the *Management* magazine, the flagship magazine for KIM, we knew each other relatively well enough for her to intervene.

"It's nice to meet you here, sir, even though it is under these stressful circumstances, sir," she said. "I just want to share with you the fact that I have a friend who has a child with a similar condition like your child's. I was with her in Moi University, School of Journalism. If you would like to talk to her I can give you her number!"

I turned with hope. "A child like ours?"

"Yes! My friend is called Anne Ngugi. She's a TV personality. Would you like to talk to her?"

Eunice and I nodded.

Carol gave us the number, then, just as fast as she had come, she retreated and was gone.

As soon as she left, I dialed Anne's number and introduced myself. I told her about her friend who had just given us her number and asked her to share her experiences with us. I knew she detected the desperation in my voice because as much as the doctor had just said all would be well, I had heard those words too many times to believe they meant anything. I felt a strong sense that as a mother who had dealt with this painful situation Anne would instantly feel our pain and help us walk a path she had already walked with her child. So when she agreed to meet me later that evening at Nairobi West, it was a welcome relief. It marked the first time I was going to know what to expect.

But was I prepared for what Anne would tell me? Was it wise to bring Eunice along to a discussion that might break her heart into tiny little pieces? Fearing that Anne's revelations might indeed be too painful to handle, I asked Eunice to let me go alone. I would tell her what Anne and I discussed when I got home, I said. Eunice didn't object. So we went back home and I went to work. My meeting with Anne would be later in the evening.

But even from work I kept calling home to find out if the corrective procedure had started to have an impact. Was Judy's head's circumference noticeably reducing? I asked.

Was she getting better?

Eunice said, "Give her a chance to heal!"

Of course I wanted to give her a chance to heal, but why was it taking so long? Why weren't the procedures having immediate impact? Did the doctors really know what they were doing or were they mere masqueraders? My reasoning was that if what had been done was corrective, Eunice should have started seeing signs of healing, right?

So what was taking so long?

———

Anne Ngugi is one of Kenya's most celebrated TV anchors. Known and admired by adoring fans as the face behind the most compelling *Kiswahili* coverage on KTN during some of Kenya's most profound occasions, you would never know that behind the grace she brings to screens across Kenya is the pain of a young mother who has spent sleepless nights crying and praying for her daughter, Angel. I met her with friends at Nairobi West; at around 5:00 p.m. It was a relief to finally meet her and pick her brains on what could help Eunice and I take care of Judy better.

The medium-height, slender anchor of KTN is a down-to-earth, welcoming mother who sees in all Kenyans a brother or a sister.

I would love to give you a detailed description of her professional excellence, but that won't be necessary for this narrative; suffice it to say that Anne has captured the imagination of many Kenyan viewers because of the way she handles herself on and off the set.

"Let's talk here," Anne told me with the warm smile that has brought cheer to many Kenyans when she anchors. "Hope you've had a good day?"

"As good as could be, Anne."

And now let me surprise you. It was when I finally sat that I first realized who I had come to see. This was the lady many Kenyans loved to dash home to watch on KTN because her coverage of news was detailed, balanced and unafraid. Was this the Anne who had a child like mine or had the lady at the hospital made a mistake and given me a wrong number?

"You are at the right place," Anne said.

I sat with Anne and her friends. Within minutes she had offered her sympathy about our little girl and set the stage for our talks. She said that having a child like she and I had could be challenging, but could also be a source of joy and blessings. I liked her directness.

"First of all, Nick," she said, "the condition is called congenital hydrocephalous."

"Congenital hydrocephalous? It's the first time I've heard what the condition is called. How come doctors have been unable to diagnose it or tell me what it is?"

Anne was shocked that till now Eunice and I hadn't known what was ailing our daughter. Congenital hydrocephalous, she went on to explain, was a condition caused by the failure of water in the head to drain away as fast as it washed in.

That was the layman way of saying it. In a child, because the skull is tender (soft), when too much water gets into the head, the head enlarges and its circumference stretches. Left unchecked, the head can grow massive and permanently impair a child.

"Did you say a corrective surgery had to be performed on your child?" Anne asked. "What had gone wrong with the first surgery and what doctor had performed it?"

"I can't tell you what went wrong, Anne, because I don't know. All I know is that when I took the baby to Nairobi Hospital, the doctor there felt the first shunt was poorly inserted. The doctor who inserted it was a renowned neurosurgeon…"

Anne cut in. "I know him. Don't ever take your child to that man again; he is not good at all.

"When he operated on my daughter, the girl oozed puss for days, until I had to seek help.

"If I were you I would take the child to the only place I know handles hydrocephalous with satisfaction. The place is called CURE International, in Mbale, Uganda. The doctors there are great and the cost is not bad at all."

"Oh Judy," I said.

Anne's tears formed. "A girl?"

"Yes, we have a girl; the fifth in a family of girls only. Tell me, Anne, what should we expect? Will she ever be like my other daughters? Will she ever fully heal?"

Anne tried to hide her forming tears, but I saw them. She didn't want to break my heart by saying something negative, so she looked down, then rather than answer, she said, "Nick, Judy's life will greatly enrich your own life. The journey will be long and sometimes painful, but I know one thing. That if you are a Christian and you are able to see everything that happens in life through the inner eye of faith, you will see in Judy an angel placed in your hands to bless you!"

Inner eyes of faith? Wasn't that supposed to be my line? I looked at Anne with amazement, not because I hadn't expected her to be a brilliant journalist, but because she had just given me more information than all the doctors I had been to their offices had given me. I was encouraged by the way she brought her faith into handling her child. As I finally got up to leave, she gave me a little present for Judy and told me to feel free to call her whenever I had a question.

Looking back today, it is clear to me that Anne was the instrument the Lord used to point Eunice and I in the right direction, because even though we took Judy to Kijabe Hospital instead of going straight to Uganda, we later followed

God's voice, spoken softly and with a smile through Anne, and took the girl to Cure International.

*

It is because of Anne Ngugi's character that my family watches any network she goes to. When she was at KTN we watched her. When she went to K24 we followed her there. We don't watch her because she is a star, though we feel she is the best, but for an entirely different reason. It is because Anne lives with an angel and has shared the story of her early days of pain, and her later days of acceptance of Angel's condition, with the world. Because of her strength of character and bravery as a mother of a special child, people like Eunice and I can look forward to a less traumatic future for our children afflicted by congenital hydrocephalous.

Seven

Judy Goes To Kijabe

Sleeping peacefully on the sunken escarpment of the Rift Valley, some sixty five kilometers northeast of Nairobi, is a town most Kenyans have only heard of by name, but have never visited. Among the many towns in the country, Kijabe has the distinction of being one of the few that go back to the days of the colonialists; and among the few that saw Kenya's earliest railway pass through it. In the eighties, it distinguished itself as the town that preached the good news and brought soothing gospel music to many through the Biblia Husema Studios, a Christian radio network started by Bob and Lillian Davis. Kijabe has given Kenya great schools like Moffat Bible College and Rift Valley Academy. It is also home to a thriving denominational press and a hospital run by the AIC Church. It was to this AIC Mission Hospital that Eunice and I decided to take Judy instead of taking her to Uganda right away, as Anne had suggested. As you will later see, that was a colossal error in judgment.

The idea of going to Kijabe started just like a joke. It is indeed amazing how ideas are easily accepted when one is desperate. By this time, we were ready to try anything and were open to any new ideas; so when a colleague heard us lament our lack of funds yet we were at the Nairobi Hospital, she advised us to leave the expensive hospital immediately and take Judy to Kijabe Hospital. She said that Kijabe had an excellent hospital run by a church and it wasn't anywhere near as expensive as Nairobi Hospital was. We had already been asked to raise 250,000.00 shillings for any form of treatment to commence; money we couldn't raise even if we were given a month to do so. Fearing, therefore, that the eventual fee would be too high to manage, we decided right there and then that we would go to Kijabe. It was a spur-of-the-moment decision that caught folks at the hospital off-guard, but there was nothing they could do to stop us. The decision was ours.

That sunny afternoon, we left Nairobi Hospital and drove down Uhuru Highway, then on to Waiyaki Way. Within an hour of our departure, we rolled into the Limuru area and sped past it toward the Kiambu County hospital, where a colleague felt help awaited us. I knew that our going to Kijabe was a compromise between doing nothing and going to Uganda; we just didn't want to go to Uganda. Like many Kenyans, we felt there was nothing Uganda really had to offer that Kenya couldn't. Wasn't Kenya East Africa's regional superpower? Weren't all the best hospitals located in Nairobi? And weren't the highest qualified doctors, men and women who had trained in the best medical schools abroad, right here in Nairobi? So why go to Uganda?

But something told me we were making a mistake. I kept hearing this soft voice warning me that going to Kijabe rather than to Uganda was a mistake. The voice kept telling me that Anne was right; that we should take Judy to Mbale, where her five-year-old child had gotten help and was now living a relatively normal life. But we didn't have the luxury of time. Judy's head was growing bigger and her crying was too painful to ignore, so Kijabe it had to be. I could see that Eunice's mind was just as made up as mine. She was resolute and determined to save her daughter—her fifth girl.

We rolled into the sleepy town at the bottom of the Rift Valley with much hope. For one, the hospital was run by Christians, which meant Christ was at the center of healing. For two, my colleague had promised that the Kijabe doctors were excellent and would get Judy out of her misery. So in spite my fear that I had ducked Mbale for now, I still felt good about things. And if this wasn't God's leading, it would become evident pretty soon by the way matters evolved.

"To begin treatment, you'll need to deposit thirty thousand shillings," we were told when we got to Kijabe.

We paid the money.

Founded in 1915 by missionaries from the Africa Inland Mission and initially named Theodora Hospital, after the U.S. President Theodore Roosevelt, the hospital runs, perhaps, East Africa's busiest operating theater and has made it its critical plank to keep costs as low as is practical. Going by the slogan Healthcare To God's Glory, this escarpment hospital aims to provide healing to Kenya's most vulnerable and has attracted patients from as far away as halfway across Africa. With a vibrant chapel and a staff of local and international experts, it is easy to see why my colleague felt the help we needed was just sixty five kilometers northwest of where we were. My initial assessment, after we were asked for the little money, and after seeing children affected by the same condition as Judy was, was that we were at the right place. We would find help here!

Judy was immediately admitted and she was prepared for the eventual surgery on her head, which took place in two days. What the doctor did was to add another shunt to the one that had been inserted at Mater by the cantankerous doctor. She now had two shunts. We stayed in Kijabe for a week and enjoyed the services there. What later disappointed us, though, was that the spot where Judy was operated on developed pus— and two weeks into her discharge, her right side got paralyzed.

I can't say her paralysis was a result of her Kijabe operation, but it left us wondering whether going straight to Mbale would have saved us this new agony. It made us feel terrible!

And matters were not helped by Anne's continuous prodding that we take Judy to Mbale. She was convinced that ultimately Judy would be taken there, so why wait?

But we waited. We lingered between opinions. Later, when it was evident that Judy's head was neither shrinking nor her crying stopping, we decided that the time had come to finally go to Uganda. As you can imagine, by this time our faith had been tested in ways only a person who has traveled this path could understand. We had prayed, cried, spent money and were now exhausted, yet nothing seemed to change; if anything we appeared to be going in circles and our urgency only served to yield one blow after another. When would this end?

——

Before we went to Uganda, friends who sensed how distressed we were financially felt a need to help us raise some money. Since the beginning of the painful journey, we had spent money in the millions and there was no end in sight to such spending. I look back now and wonder where the money came from, because it couldn't have possibly come from my salary or the paltry twenty thousand shillings folks in the village had sent us to manage the crisis.

So one sunny evening, right there in downtown Nairobi, at the Professional Center, off Parliament Road, friends and relatives gathered to help us raise funds toward Judy's treatment.

Before the collections started, as is usually the practice, Eunice and I narrated the story of Judy's illness and her own illness before giving birth. We told the gathering how painful it had been, but also reminded them of the power of their prayers and friendship.

Among the guests we invited to play a leading role in fundraising was Reuben Ndinya, Sarah Serem, Sylas Simatwo and Edward Bitok, four selfless friends who galvanized folks and donated more money than we had anticipated.

We remain indebted to them and all friends and relatives who participated in that drive. It left us feeling light about the burden we had borne for so long.

A few days after that fundraiser, I called Anne Ngugi and told her we were taking Judy to Uganda. I still remember how excited she was that this was finally happening. Because of her experience with hydrocephalous and the pain it caused the child and parents, she was eager to see us get immediate help. She wished us well and said she would be praying for us!

*

Eunice and I have been members of the Nairobi East Church for many years. There, we have made friends and regard brothers and sisters in the church as family. The church is located just off Jogoo Road, a couple of miles from Nairobi's bustling CBD. In this church, we have prayed with brothers and sisters in distress; those who have lost loved ones and even those who have had patients in hospitals. This time it was our turn to be ministered to. The prospect of going to Uganda was at once as exciting as it was troubling. There was fear and hope; a sense that if things didn't go wrong they would go right. That's why we called the brethren to pray with us.

By this time Pastor Guto, who we had constantly briefed on our progress, or lack of it, was in no mood to play games with the devil. He felt, and rightly so, that this illness had gone on too long and God needed to deliver us. So he led the gathered prayer warriors in a prayer of dedication for Judy and our family. He pleaded with God to let us come back from Uganda with the good news of Judy's healing. With his normally calm voice breaking, the man of God asked the Master to plant angles ahead of us, behind us and on the sides. By the time folks said amen, I felt something. I felt renewal of hope and a sense that this was the beginning of Judy's healing. Eunice too, later she told me, felt the same thing. If this was God's way of finally getting us on a path to our daughter's healing, we were going to Uganda with tremendous hope. We knew that the Lord who had once split the Jordan so that the Israelites could go free; Him who had fed five thousand hungry folks on two loaves of bread and five fish; that same lion of Judah who once walked on water and never drowned… we knew that He was just waiting for us to realize that He was able. And now we had.

So was Uganda going to heal Judy? That we didn't know; what we knew for sure was that God had already traveled ahead of us and was waiting for us in Mbale.

Eight

Judy's First Foreign Trip

The Republic of Uganda is a landlocked country in East Africa. It is bordered on the east by Kenya, on the north by South Sudan, on the west by the Democratic Republic of the Congo, on the southwest by Rwanda, and on the south by Tanzania. The southern part of the country includes a substantial portion of Lake Victoria, shared with Kenya and Tanzania, situating the country in the African Great Lakes region. Uganda also lies within the Nile basin, and has a varied but generally equatorial climate, which makes it a wonderful place to live.

Uganda takes its name from the dominant Buganda kingdom, which encompasses a large portion of the south of the country including the emerging capital Kampala. The people of Uganda were hunter-gatherers until about 1,700 to 2,300 years ago, when Bantu-speaking populations migrated to the southern parts of the country. May I continue?

Beginning in the late 1800s, the area was ruled as a colony by the British, who established administrative law across the territory. Uganda gained independence from Britain on the 9th of October 1962. The period since then has been marked by intermittent conflicts, most recently a lengthy civil war against the Lord's Resistance Army, which has caused tens of thousands of casualties and displaced more than a million people—under the leadership of Kony.

The official language is English. Luganda, a central language, is widely spoken across the country, and multiple other languages are also spoken including Swahili. The current President of Uganda is Yoweri Kaguta Museveni, who came to power in a coup in 1986. That's my calibrated history of the nation Anne had suggested we take Judy to.

You may clap for me now!

We left Nairobi with Eunice and Judy in a bus. It was Kampala Coach. In the bus, Eunice and I took turns watching over Judy, who spent most of the night asleep. She was about seven months old then. When we got to Eldoret, we teamed up with my younger brother, Elkana, who had been very supportive and had prayed for Judy's healing as if she were his own. Elkana had insisted on coming with us to see for himself how his favorite niece was treated and how Eunice and I held up under the strain of our situation. Because of his coming along, we now had three hands to handle Judy as we traveled. The ride to Malava, the border, was quiet. If things proceeded according to plan, we would be in Mbale about midday, a great time to arrive at the hospital.

As we traveled, we reminisced over the past and talked about the tremendous pressure Judy's illness had exerted on the family. We observed that Eunice, who had always been a reserved lady, had become even less talkative, but a lot more prayerful; if that were ever possible. I, on the other hand, having been more of an extrovert, had become even more expressive and upfront with Judy's condition whenever I met friends, relatives, colleagues and any person who could offer help. My upfront attitude was driven by a desire to remove stigma from the child and to find the quickest, surest way to help my daughter out of this situation. As for Elkana, we noted that even though we had been close brothers, Judy's condition had drawn us a lot closer and now we relied on each other a lot more for strength.

"And how has Judy affected her sisters?" I finally asked Eunice as the bus approached Jinja.

Eunice painted a moving picture of the girls. She said the girls had all been affected by the ongoing struggles of their sister. Janet had made it a point to always be there to help whenever she was needed, while the other girls had said private prayers for Judy, as Mama had told them to do. On more than one occasion, I found one or the other of the girls on their knees praying. In such moments, I walked away without telling them I had seen them on their knees because I didn't want them to see my forming tears. It was obvious to me that whoever came into Judy's world left profoundly impacted by her young life. She had touched folks at church, at our office, at the hospitals and even at home. Judy's world was a place of pain and happiness; a zone of weakness and strength; the only place in this world where you went to find God in the middle of confusion.

When we got to Jinja, the bus stopped for a break. As Elkana and I stepped out to stretch, I told him about the town and its origins. This town in eastern Uganda is known more for the River Nile than for its arresting beauty and horrific history during the brutal reign of Idi Amin Dada. The River Nile has its source right here in Jinja, where it begins its startling journey into Egypt to the north, wading through Sudan and other territories before it splits into the Egyptian tributaries of Damietta and Rosetta. When you visit the source of the Nile, you will be amazed by the wonders of nature. The Nile is as attractive as it is scary. Just thinking about it, it was hard for Elkana, as it had been for me when I first read about the River Nile, to comprehend that the waters now in Uganda would eventually end up in the Mediterranean Sea, thousands of miles away from where we were now.

Moments later, the bus drove off and we sped toward Mukono, and eventually rolled into the city of Kampala.

Around 8:00 a.m., we left Kampala for Mbale. On this ride, we were slated to cover some 245 kilometers. The town is the administrative capital of Mbale District and lies to the northeast of Kampala on an all-weather tarmac road. It sits astride the Tororo-Pakwach railway line. Mount Elgon, one of East Africa's highest peaks, is close by as well. As we arrived in this eastern town, a pensive mood descended on the three of us. We couldn't immediately tell what awaited us in Mbale and at the hospital called CURE International. I couldn't help but wonder afresh why we'd had to travel to this country to seek treatment for Judy when such treatment should have been available in Kenya. Why did this have to happen?

———

CURE International, one of the greatest ideas to emerge out of missionary activities in Africa, is a nonprofit organization based in Lemoyne, Pennsylvania. CURE's efforts are focused on providing medical care to children suffering primarily from orthopedic conditions. The organization's stated mission is "healing the sick and proclaiming the kingdom of God."

The organization was founded in 1996 by Dr. Scott Harrison and his wife, Sally. Ten years earlier, Dr. Harrison traveled to Malawi, Africa, to perform spine surgery and teach higher level orthopedic surgery skills to local surgeons. In the years following, Dr. Harrison and his wife made many trips back, discovering a need to care for children with orthopedic disabilities.

When his tenure as CEO and President of Kirschner Medical was over, Dr. Harrison created CURE, hoping to meet that need. CURE's first hospital opened in 1998 in Kenya. Since then, CURE has seen approximately 2,100,000 patients, performed approximately 150,000 surgeries, and trained approximately 6,600 national medical professionals. Today, it is the largest provider of pediatric surgical care in the developing world.

By coming to this hospital, Judy was about to count herself as one among the millions of patients to have been treated by the kind men and women at CURE International. When we arrived, the lady who received us told us what to expect. One, there would be no down payment; Judy would be seen—at least in these initial stages—for free. We were pleasantly surprised by this gesture. Second, only Eunice would stay with the child in the ward once admitted; Elkana and I had to find a place to stay in Mbale as we lingered in the town to monitor Judy's progress.

"What else?" I asked the lady, already delighted by these unexpectedly favorable terms.

"That will be it for now!"

And so Judy was finally at the place Anne had wanted her to be. She was now in the hands of the folks at CURE International. She was admitted by Dr. Mugambi, an amazing surgeon who wondered why in the world the folks at Kijabe had stitched Judy's head after her procedure. His misgivings were as a result of the fact that in Mbale they used special glue and not stitch. After a careful assessment of the situation, he admitted Judy, then Elkana and I left to find a place to spend the night. Over the next week, Judy was treated in Mbale and we remained there in prayer, hope and war against evil.

Two days after our arrival, Dr. Mugambi performed a delicate surgery on Judy's head and replaced the two shunts that were now in our girl's head. The procedure was called Endoscopic Third Ventriculostomy (ETV). This being the third surgery, I wanted to know what caused the condition and whether Judy would one day completely heal. True to his reputation, the doctor told Eunice and I what to expect and warned us to be prepared to nurture a child with hydrocephalous. "This will be your life from now on," he said candidly, looking at us in turns.

"Will she be able to walk?"

"Yes," he said.

"Eat alone?"

"Yes!"

"Shower?"

"With help!"

"Go to school?"

Dr. Mugambi drew a deep breath. "Let me say it this way. It will be your choice whether and what school Judy goes to. Some parents have elected to take their children to special schools; others have elected to take them to formal schools. I don't know what advantage one has over the other, but I hope studies now underway will shed light on this soon enough. So I leave that decision to Eunice and you."

Eunice said, "Will she be able to talk?"

Dr. Mugambi nodded. "She will. She will even sing!"

We were happy to hear that. Do you want to know why? It was because in spite of Judy's condition, which was now made worse by her paralysis, she would be able to do certain basic things. Under our calibrated expectations, we couldn't ask for more. We were ready to take whatever the Lord gave us!

*

A week after we arrived in Mbale, Dr. Mugambi discharged Judy and we left the hospital hopeful that the end of our misery had come. If nothing extraordinary or unexpected happened, we would come back for a regular checkup in three months, then six months, then in a year.

But the devil was not ready to let us off the hook yet, so rather than let Judy's healing proceed on schedule, he caused the shunt to block, which made Judy's head enlarge again and her crying to reach fever pitch. In the face of such horror, I found myself asking whether going to Uganda had been a wise move or a waste of time.

**

Fearing that the blockage could cause lasting damage, we decided to take Judy back to Mbale. But this time it was Elkana and Eunice who went.

Nine

Back To Mbale

On the day Eunice and Elkana went back to Mbale, Elkana kept calling to give me updates on what was going on. He told me about their arrival in Malava, in Kampala and in Mbale. And finally, when treatment started, he informed me what the doctor had done. He made it easy for Eunice, who had to worry about the minute-by-minute details of what was going on and couldn't be available to update me. Later that night, as I waited for sleep to clump my eyes, I thought about my years in primary school. My teachers at Itigo, especially Mr. Elisha Odhiambo, had trained me well and saw to it that I was among the students accepted at the prestigious Kapsabet Boys High School. In my first term at Kapsabet I ended up in position three and I never looked back.

At the time I was in Itigo Primary School, Eunice, a girl four years younger than me, was under the care of her grandparents in Kipkabus, near Burnt forest. Later, when I was in Kapsabet Boys, where Mr. John Peter Mackenzie forged a close relationship with the then President Daniel arap Moi to drive the school to the top in excellence, Eunice went to Ngeria Secondary School, not too far from her home. I didn't know her and she didn't know me; because the year we would meet was still ahead.

It was while there, at Kapsabet Boys High School, that the man I would one day become started to emerge. I made friends with a Luhya gentleman called Reuben Ndinya Khamadi, a highly driven guy who never settled for less than the best. Together, we decided that nothing was going to stop us from achieving our dreams. What we didn't know then was what those dreams were.

Enter Mr. Thomas Musau.

Mr. Musau was our career teacher. Together with the Principal, who looked into matters of our future like we were his own children, we followed the advice of Mr. Musau. The man claimed he had seen in us students of commerce. I salute the late Mr. Musau, who died in a road accident later, for having seen the potential in us and set us on a path to success.

I studied commerce, together with Reuben, and we made it to the University of Nairobi. There, we formed a powerful study group comprising of: Daniel Mutahi, Beatrice Kamiri, George Wachiuri, Reuben Ndinya Khamadi, Rose Kilemi, Mary Okello and I. We later graduated and...

The phone rang.

"Hello?"

It was Elkana. "This didn't take very long," he said. "The doctor has advised that we be here for three days so he can observe Judy."

"How is she?" I asked.

"Judy is okay. She seems better than when we came."

"And Eunice?"

"Tired."

"Why didn't you call earlier?"

Elkana explained that he had tried to call, but there were network problems. I thanked him and advised him to sleep at the same place we had slept a couple of days ago. Three days later, Judy was brought back home by the mother and her uncle. She seemed okay and I was delighted to see that the blockage had not caused any more damage than could be handled by Dr. Mugambi and his team at CURE International. But a week after Judy came back, we noted the blockage again. This time I got so dispirited that I found myself wondering whether there was something I, as a father, or Eunice, as a mother, had done to cause so much pain to our child. Was God punishing us for something we didn't know about?

If He was, why had He refused to forgive us in spite of the prayers of His servants at church—and even our own fervent prayers? What did He want from us?

Even Eunice, who had all along been a formidable fortress of faith, wondered why the Lord had allowed so much grief to come our way.

But determined not to let this second blockage destroy our will to find lasting healing for Judy, we decided that we would go to Gertrude's Children's Hospital. I told Anne about this decision and she agreed that it was okay to try whatever was available. She was at a loss as to what may have caused the two blockages because this was new to her. We kept the faith, however, and even managed to think about the good times our family had been through.

"Remember when you told me to go to Baraton?" Eunice asked the night before Judy was due to be taken to Gertrude's.

"I told you I couldn't handle school anymore, but you insisted I give it a shot."

"Yes, you owe me!" I said.

"I went to Baraton just fine, and even made the Dean's List. I later went on to the University of Nairobi after having our first four daughters and graduated with my MBA on the very day you graduated with your PhD. Do you know how hard it was to study when I was a mother, a wife and a worker?

"It felt like climbing a mountain with a rock tied to my back!"

"It's true. I still wonder how you did it." I cleared my throat.

"That's why I believe no adversity will ever overcome us, especially when we place our faith where it has always been— in the God who created the heavens and the earth."

"So you think Gertrude's is a wise decision? You don't want us to go back to CURE?" she asked.

I said, "Let's give Gertrude's a chance, after all it's a children's hospital just like CURE. You never know, we might just find healing there."

On that note, we slept, but I remained awake for a while. In the hours my eyes refused to shut, I talked to God about my family.

I discussed the pain Eunice had been through as the mother of a hydrocephalic child; the agony our daughters had endured as the children of worried parents; the body blows I had absorbed with each news of no progress on Judy's healing. I asked God to bring this bitter cup to an end and allow the weary family to find peace. It was all I could ask before the Lord blew his Spirit of peace into me and I slept like a little baby till morning.

———

In the time that Judy's world was becoming our world, I had finished my masters degree and had finally defended my doctoral dissertation. My career was on the right path—and Eunice was ready to enroll into her masters program at the University of Nairobi. It sometimes made me wonder whether, like the Apostle Paul's eye irritant, this was something the Lord had allowed to happen so we would always be kept humble in the face of His blessings. When I asked Eunice about that possibility, she thought about it, then nodded.

I said, "Does that mean Judy keeps us humble?"

"Of course she does. Judy is the eyes through which we see the unconditional love of God; the fingers by which we touch and feel God's grace." She gave my hand a gentle rub, then added,

"Actually, Judy is our reminder of the cross!"

Though I hadn't thought about Judy and the powerful image of the cross, I exaggeratedly nodded, then said, "You're so right. Judy is our family's link to compassion. On the coming Day of Judgment, the Lord will overlook a lot of what we have done in this world, but He will not overlook what we will have done with the least of these!"

Ten

At Gertrude's: Judy In A Coma

The city of Nairobi, and indeed our great nation, owes Colonel Grogan a tremendous debt of gratitude on behalf of the rising generation. Not only is the hospital his gift to the children of East Africa, but his personal interest, drive and perseverance have been largely instrumental in thrashing the way through all the regulations and controls which make construction work such a nightmare to the ordinary citizen. The hospital was founded in 1947 with the donation of land by Colonel Ewart Grogan in memory of his wife, Gertrude.

As the years go by, Gertrude's Hospital has become more and more of a 'giving' hospital. It has won prestigious awards for its Corporate Social Responsibility (CSR). This hospital, right from the beginning, was and will always be a simple hospital. It has completed the full circle by becoming a place of hope for sick children who have no expectations elsewhere; which was what Grogan had desired deeply for the London orphans.

For an organization that began sixty years ago with a small staff and only sixteen beds, Gertrude's is now able to offer a genuine one-stop pediatric center that can provide almost every available treatment a child might need. It was to this storied nonprofit organization (hospital), that I brought Judy when it seemed like we had hit another brick wall in Mbale. Eunice and I came to this hospital without too much hope. In fact our coming had nothing to do with treatment; it had everything to do with mollifying our conscience that we had done something to alleviate Judy's suffering.

Over the past couple of days, before our coming to Gertrude's, Judy's shunt had blocked again and this time it wasn't just another block; it had caused her crying to increase threefold and even made her vomit. Her voice was shrill, pestering and urgent. If Judy had ever needed lightning-speed help, this time was it, so there was no time to waste. As the day broke, we knew we had to answer two questions right away. One, could we make it back to Uganda? Two, was this the end? This second question was prompted in our minds by the words of a certain doctor who had told us to prepare for the worst. The worst was death. I recalled those words with trepidation. Could this be the way God had designed Judy's end to happen?

Arriving at the Muthaiga Gertrude's Hospital, which was also the administrative nerve of the Gertrude's chain of hospitals, we were handled with speed and certain checking in preliminaries were overlooked because the girl was in deep distress. It wasn't long before a doctor was summoned to take care of Judy. As this went on, I retreated to a corner and started pleading with God again.

Fear washed over me because even with my untrained eye, I could see that Judy was slipping away. I could tell that Eunice too felt the troubling signs of a mother about to part with a child. Of all the moments I had faced since this dark cloud started passing over our heads, this was the one time I felt my knees wobble and my tears flow unabated.

And even though I pulled away to hide them from Eunice, I knew she sensed that I was crying. The pain finally became too much to bear. Praying there, I asked God why this ordeal had to be prolonged. Why had He let a little child suffer such bitter agony not of her making?

When would He find it necessary to come down and end this? Hadn't I pleaded with him to forgive any sin Eunice or I might have committed so that Judy could go free? Why was He hiding His face?

Eunice came over to me. "They are about to start a procedure on Judy. Do you want to be there as they do it?"

I turned slowly. "I want to," I said.

Eunice looked at me and I saw her tears form. "You've been crying? I thought you were praying!"

I looked at Eunice and for the first time wondered whether there was s difference between prayer and tears. When a man cries, I wondered, doesn't the Lord know what he's distressed about? Aren't tears a language the Lord understands?

"She's really in a bad shape, isn't she?" Eunice asked.

I nodded, but didn't talk.

We left my little corner and went to the room, where the doctor said, "We have to remove the shunt and insert another through the same kind of surgery Judy has faced four times in the hands of different doctors."

"Why?" I demanded. "What's wrong with this one? All I can let you do is unblock it, but that's it, because…"

He cut in. "It needs to be replaced."

In spite of my misgivings, I let the doctor carry out a surgery to unblock the shunt. That was all I was willing to let the doctors here do because I wasn't happy with their approach to matters of life and death. He unblocked the shunt, but two weeks later nothing appeared to be working and we got thoroughly disillusioned. Meanwhile, Judy's condition deteriorated steadily. We watched, each passing day, as her skin became flabby, her skin color became dull and the sense heightened that if we didn't act with speed we would lose our daughter.

"I feel the time has now come for us to replace that shunt," the doctor said one afternoon, sweeping in with the confidence of a maestro before mesmerizing a spellbound audience with breathless classical renditions. "An operation to replace the shunt is our only bet!"

I refused. By now my confidence in the Kenyan doctors was so low that gambling with Judy's life was not an option. From the nasty experience with the neurosurgeon at Mater to the paralyzed right side of Judy, which we feared was as a result of another careless surgical procedure in the hands of a Kenyan doctor, I didn't want to place my daughter's life in the hands of these careless men and women. It seemed to me like they were all in a mad rush to make quick money, not to treat patients with the care and dignity they deserved. And though I feared that Judy needed urgent help, I didn't want that help to come from folks to whom her life was measured in shillings, not in the painful agony of her mother and father.

Eunice pulled me aside and said, "What are you doing?"

"I don't want them to remove that shunt here!"

"But our child may di… Sorry, so where do you want us to take Judy now? What are we going to do?"

At that very second, as if the world of dark forces had pinned my back to the wall, the doctor walked to us and warned that we didn't have very much time. That a decision needed to be reached at once so that the child could get help. "Sir, are we proceeding or not?" he prodded.

I said no.

"Let me explain something to you, sir," he said. "If your daughter doesn't have that shunt replaced, I doubt she will make it. This is urgent!"

But I stood my ground and the doctor left Eunice and I consulting. Moments later, his face grim and his voice breaking, the doctor whispered that Judy had slipped into a coma. To help you understand what a coma is, let me tell you what *Wikipedia* says about the situation: In medicine, a coma—from the Greek κῶμα *koma*, meaning "deep sleep"—is a state of unconsciousness lasting more than six hours, in which a person: cannot be awakened; fails to respond normally to painful stimuli, light, or sound; lacks a normal sleep-wake cycle;

and does not initiate voluntary actions. A person in a state of coma is described as being comatose.

A comatose person exhibits a complete absence of wakefulness and is unable to consciously feel, speak, hear, or move. For a patient to maintain consciousness, two important neurological components must function. The first is the cerebral cortex— the gray matter that covers the outer layer of the brain. The other is a structure located in the brainstem called reticular activating system (RAS). Injury to either or both of these components is sufficient to cause a patient to experience a coma. The cerebral cortex is a group of tight, dense, "gray matter" composed of the nucleus of the neurons whose axons then form the "white matter", and is responsible for perception, relay of the sensory input (sensation) via the thalamic pathway, and many other neurological functions, including complex thinking. If you don't understand that stuff, don't blame yourself, I don't either. Because I didn't, the doctor told me in layman terms that as things stood now, Judy was in a state of deep sleep. She could not see, talk, understand or even conceive of anything.

"So can we replace the shunt?" the doctor demanded, his confusion about my refusal causing him to wonder about my sanity. "Can we save the girl?"

Right there, as Eunice's tears flowed and my hands trembled with the cold fear of making a decision I knew could haunt me forever, I shook my head a final time and told the doctor to discharge my daughter.

"You're making a grave mistake," he fired.

Eunice said, "Why are we doing this?"

"Because we are going back to Uganda!"

"Uganda? But the child is in a coma!"

Yes, she was in a coma, and yes I knew that should she die Eunice would hold me responsible for my inexplicable decision, but this I had to do. I had prayed about it and the Lord had made it clear to me what I needed to do, so I wasn't gonna go back on it.

"Then let's do this," the doctor finally said, his head shaking in disbelief. "But if that baby has to leave this hospital, I want you to sign a statement releasing us from any liability should she die.

Are you willing to do that?"

"I am. Get the papers ready for me to sign!"

With my hand shaking and Eunice watching me in disbelief, I held the black pen, fought back tears and scribbled my signature on the document the doctor had placed before me. With that one act, I had stated that if Judy died, which there was every likelihood of, I was going to be the only one responsible for the death because neither Eunice nor the hospital authorities could be blamed.

Realizing that time was now of the essence, I called Elkana and asked him to prepare for another trip to Mbale. That evening, when we left that hospital, I looked back at my life to figure out where the courage I had exhibited at the hospital had come from, because even though my father was in the General Service Unit, I couldn't have taken my courage from him; he was someone I never lived with much. I could also have never taken that courage from my mother; Mama Truphena Lelei was a retiring homemaker who was happy just to see that her children went to school and Papa was kept happy. So this had nothing to do with my courage; it had something to do with fatalism borne of faith in a higher being. This wasn't Nicholas acting; it was God!

We left the hospital with Judy in a coma and Eunice in a state of panic. I had just done something I knew she had never seen me do before—act irresponsible or fanatical. To Eunice, and to our children, I was a common sense dad, who everyone looked up to for calm decision-making. Eunice had never seen me act so reckless and with such unwavering conviction. So as we made our way out the main entrance and finally the gate, she kept her lips zipped and appeared to have resigned to whatever may befall us. And even though I knew she was dying to ask whether I had given up on Judy, I also refrained from saying anything. There's a time to talk and a time to be quiet; a time to sing and a time to cry; a time to be brave and a time to collapse at the foot of Calvary. For me, the time to have this burden lifted at Calvary had come. God was now in control!

———

Four hours after we left Gertrude's Hospital, Eunice and I made it to Jomo Kenyatta International Airport and settled into a Kenya Airways jet to Eldoret International Airport, about ten kilometers from our Mosoriot home. But before we did so, I called my father-in-law, Elder Samuel Nyango, a respected Megun Church Elder; and a couple of folks at home to pray with us. It was in that brief call that we agreed to have a major prayer session for Judy when we came back from Uganda. For some reason, even though I knew the dire situation we were in, I felt as if leaving this matter in the hands of God was the right thing to do; God was fully in control now.

*

You can just imagine what happened when we got to Mbale and Dr. Mugambi realized Judy was in a coma!

Eleven

Mugambi's Prayerful Touch

There is a song Eunice and I love to sing when the burdens of life overwhelm us. Many times before, we have sung the song at our family worship and enjoyed the lyrics because they sound sweet to the ear when sung aloud and melodiously. But this noon hour, as Eunice and Elkana and I came through the gate of CURE International, I didn't have the nerve or the voice to sing aloud; all I could do was sing the song in my heart. As I did, I felt, for the first time in my life, what it meant to sing. I felt the song, felt the pain of its writer and felt the relief that settled over him like a dove when he realized that *Burdens are Lifted at Calvary*!

The song was written in 1952 by a Baptist pastor called John M. Moore. At the time he wrote the song, he was serving as the assistant superintendent of the Seaman's Chapel, in Glasgow, Scotland. What happened was, someone called the Seaman's Chapel and requested that Pastor Moore gets to one of the Glasgow hospitals, where a seaman lay critically ill.

The pastor, in a hurry, went to the hospital and found the young man on the verge of death. He talked to the young seaman for a while, then shoved his hand into his case to pull out a tract—not knowing which one would come out. The one that came out was based on the Pilgrim's Progress!

The pilgrim had a burden on his back!

Pastor Moore told the young seaman a brief story of the burdened pilgrim, then went on to identify with him by saying that the pilgrim's experience had been his too. Like the pilgrim, Pastor Moore said, his life was full of burden until he took that burden to the cross and left it there. It was then, he said, that he felt like his sin and guilt was removed. When he asked the seaman whether he also wanted his sin and guilt removed, the young seaman nodded and they prayed together. He left the seaman smiling, his burden lifted.

Later that night, sitting by a fireside, Pastor Moore grabbed a paper and pen and wrote this song that was going to bless folks around the world.

I bring you this amazing story because as Eunice and I entered the gates of the Mbale-based hospital, the song did for me something that had not happened since the beginning of Judy's illness—it brought me peace. I sung it in my heart with so much cheer and meaning, assured tho the God who had created Judy was the same God who had lifted the burdens of His children through the years. No, there was nothing to fear anymore. If it was His decision that Judy had only come to be with us for a few months—or maybe a year—I was now ready to accept His will. I was ready to give Judy back to Him who knew what was best for the child. And so for the first time, just before we got into Dr. Mugambi's office, I whispered a prayer and said, "Father, let your will be done!"

That prayer was my moment of faith. It was the moment I felt the burden of the last couple of months lift; not because I had said let whatever happens happen, but because I had finally taken my burden to the cross and left it with God.

From there on, I wasn't going to worry, cry or pray with conditions to the Master; I was going to live my life on the basis that my name was clear before my father and Judy was His child.

"Another block? Does that mean the ETV wasn't successful?" Dr. Mugambi asked as soon as he saw us.

I said, "Yes, Doc; and Judy is in a coma!"

The doctor literally jumped to his feet and hurried to Judy. And even though he appeared stoic, I saw tears form in his eyes as he looked at Eunice with sympathy. If there was anything he could do to save this poor mother further agony, I knew right there he could have done it. But as things stood, he still had to find out whether the child was indeed in a coma and whether Judy could be saved.

As he assessed Judy, I heard him repeatedly ask the little girl a question. He said: *Judy, what is eating you?* But Judy didn't say a word. She was lost in her world where only she knew what was going on. Try as I might to get into her world and see the world through her eyes and mind, I just couldn't. I didn't know whether she was in a lot of pain, out of pain, or in some pain.

The only thing that gave me comfort was that Little Judy was now in the hands of a doctor far superior to all the doctors that had attended to her. She was in the hands of a comforter far mightier than her dad and mom, who thought money could solve the world's problems. She was in the hands of a being philosophers had called omnipotent and omnipresent after failing to find adequate words to describe Him. So Dr. Mugambi didn't need to give us pity; he needed to do for Judy what her father in heaven would lead him to do. That was the substance of faith; because when man's wisdom ended, God's grace started; and that's what we needed now.

"This is what we must do," Dr. Mugambi finally said, his voice breaking with raw emotion. "I want this child to be seen by a pediatrician. This is a matter of Pediatrics."

I didn't like the idea much, but there was nothing I could do; he was the professional.

"Let me give you the pediatrician's number. You need to touch base with her right away!" he said.

I took the information and was ready to leave. Suddenly, Dr. Mugambi said, "Wait a minute. Maybe I should try one more surgery. The ETV is obviously not working. Let me open Judy up to see what could be causing problems. I don't want to make any promises, but it won't hurt to do one last surgery. Are you okay with that?"

Eunice nodded. As for me, it didn't matter anymore; this matter was now in the hands of God. If Dr. Mugambi felt, as suddenly as this thought had come to him, that he needed to do a surgery, it must have been God leading him, so I didn't need to give him permission; God had already done it. Besides, wasn't he also a prayerful doctor who we all felt was guided by God in whatever he did? That's why I felt the voice that had ambushed him and told him to try a last surgery was divine. The Lord had stepped in to do the surgery Himself; Dr. Mugambi was just but an instrument He was going to use. I felt elated. And there being no time to waste at all, immediate preparations were made to bring Judy into the Operating

Room. And so, at long last, I felt God was getting where none of us had ever managed to get into: into Judy's world. That was the place all the answers were!

———

That cloudy evening, just before Judy was wheeled into the Operating Room, Dr. Mugambi called us into his office and we prayed together. A deeply spiritual man, he was one of those doctors who believed that whatever they had achieved in life— and even the miracle of healing his patients experienced—was because of his reliance on God. It brought great joy to my heart when I heard the zeal with which he prayed for Judy. It was clear to me that he wanted nothing less than total healing for Judy. He wanted to see Judy grow up to be a playful girl, a healthy teenager and later a responsible young woman.

As I listened to him talk to God, I suddenly realized why our Kenyan doctors had failed to inspire me. It was because most of them never had a relationship with the Creator of life; and even those who did treated God as a name to be called for the sake of the patients, not for the doctors themselves.

To most Kenyan medics, God was an equal; someone only weaklings and uneducated masses believed in. No, God was an intrusion that didn't belong in medicine; He belonged in church, where ministers of the gospel used Him to fleece unsuspecting faithful. That was God to the Kenyan doctor!

I know what I've just said amounts to a sweeping statement, but it represents pretty accurately the picture. So let me make a another strident statement here: As long as medicine in Kenya remains the exclusive preserve of men and women who value money over life and have no place for the Creator of life in their practice, many more Kenyans will continue to suffer in the hands of our doctors. I will be praying that the situation changes for the sake of my fellow countrymen.

*

As the sun started its last journey of the day, dipping its nose behind the blue horizon yonder, Judy was wheeled into the Operating Room, with Eunice and Elkana and I in tow. Although I could tell that Eunice and my brother were deeply worried, I was in a totally different state of mind. In fact, I had a good feeling that this would be Judy's final surgery because this one was to be performed by the Creator. The first day of Judy's healing had come.

**

And so Judy was placed on the Operating Room table in her comatose state and the doctor flashed a forced smile at us. In that moment, I knew that the Lord was in this place. He had come to get into Judy's world!

Twelve

God's Own Touch

One of the most dramatic encounters between man and a deity in the Bible is the narrative found in the book of Genesis, where Jacob confronted God and asked Him to bless him (Jacob). Each time I read that story I'm reminded of the power of determination. Jacob wasn't just another man; he was a patriarch, a man future generations would look up to as a source of inspiration. But on this one night—a night he felt the urgent need for a blessing—he decided to do what many of us wouldn't dare do: he took on God. I want you to bless me, he said. And it wasn't like he was gentle about it; he demanded it. The narrator of the story tells of how Jacob wrestled the Lord until morning, whereupon, as it became dawn and the Lord didn't want folks to see him, He touched Jacob's hip joint and Jacob felt a pang, then he let go. But, and this is where I drew my strength from on the evening Judy faced the knife again, Jacob got the blessing he so desperately craved.

I am not Jacob and I have never wrestled God, but I know I have asked Him a few pointed questions. I'm also certain that on the day Judy was born, if God had been near me, the Nandi spirit in me would have probably sought Him and demanded the kind of blessing that would cover Eunice, Judy and our four daughters. I would have fought hard to have Him shield my family from the burdens and sorrows of life. I can imagine that my selfishness would have probably made me ask that He ensures I became one of the greatest men and that my family became prosperous in worldly ways as well as heavenly.

But this evening wealth and worldly glory was the last thing on my mind; the only thing I wanted was Judy to come out of the surgery alive and to eventually get well. That was it. I had no desire to one day proclaim my greatness because of Judy's healing; only to let the cross be my boast because of the faith that had made Judy whole. And so as Dr. Mugambi started his surgery, I sat by Eunice's side and for the first time told her why I had insisted we come to Mbale, to Dr. Mugambi.

"It was God's directive," I told her.

"God?"

"Yes. The Lord has come down to heal Judy. He is here with us today. Judy will come out of this just fine!"

"But what is different?" Eunice asked.

I explained to her the way faith works. I told her that over the past couple of months, we had relied heavily on money and man's expertise to heal Judy. The difference was that I now knew what we should have done a long time ago. "We should have left the matter in the hands of God and let Him take control. That's how we should have handled this."

"Didn't we do that through prayer?"

"We did," I said. "But after prayer we carried on as if we retained some capacity to effect the outcome we desired. It was only last night when it occurred to me that we were utterly powerless to do anything. That was why when I heard that still voice that warned me not to let Judy be operated on again at Gertrude's, in spite of Judy's grave situation, I obeyed that voice and said we had to leave."

"You never told me about this!"

"I couldn't have; there was no time. Besides, I knew you wouldn't have believed me. I thank you for making the hardest decision you've ever made since we got married—the decision to leave the hospital with a comatose child and to carry her across the border in her state of lifelessness. The fearless Nandi heroine I met at the hardware store is still in you!"

"That day I was in my father's hardware store because I had been asked to manage it. I thought you were just another of the many customers. Suddenly you walked in like you owned the world and surprised me by calling my name. You were like: How are you, Eunice?"

"And you told me that I don't speak to strangers."

Eunice laughed. It was the first time I had seen her laugh so heartily. It made me sense that she also felt a burden lift since we came back here. I told her how I later pursued her through my uncle Simon and how folks in her village had said such glowing words about her. So later, when we met in church and on our unplanned meetings in *matatus* to Eldoret, we got to know each other better and a village love blossomed in us. She loved my company and I loved hers. We carried on with the relationship until the day came when I told my parents that the time had come to talk to Eunice's parents. For me, now that I was done with my studies at the university and Eunice was done with her studies at Ngeria High school, there was nothing else to wait for. We needed to get married; and the marriage needed to be done in an orderly manner.

When the day came to meet Eunice's folks, seven elders from my village, including my father, went to Eunice's' home with seven elderly women. Usually such first encounters can go wrong when the families involved have one form of feud or another, but in our case, because of our Christian background, things went smoothly. In the coming months, dowry was sent to Eunice's home and we finally got married.

"Then we had Janet!" she said.

I knew she wanted me to talk about the rest of our daughters and the way I had taken her to Baraton and the University of Nairobi, but before I could talk, I saw a beaming, but measured Dr. Mugambi walk toward us. Since my first meeting with this man, I had never seen him so excited, which made me wonder what he was about to say. Even Eunice, who always shuddered at the incomprehensible updates of the doctors, was eager to hear what the guardedly optimistic doctor had to say.

"It's been three hours," he said, taking my hand.

"You are right," I said. Elkana joined us from where he'd been seated—or sleeping was more accurate.

"You may come see Judy, but I have to warn that she hasn't woken up yet. What I found in her head was an island of water, which is what prevented her brain systems from working well. I have drained that water and set in place a new shunt to the stomach. What we have to do now is pray that Judy will be well. I have done my best!"

But deep in my heart I knew he hadn't done a thing; this one was God's surgery. It was God's own touch. And it didn't take long for my faith to be affirmed because as we stood there, thirty minutes after Dr. Mugambi had called us in, Judy started moving her limbs and crying. That crying, which had earlier on made us shudder and seek ways to keep her quiet, was now the sweetest sound to our ears. I could see that Eunice wanted to pick her up, but Dr. Mugambi restrained her with his eyes. And suddenly, the girl who had been comatose for several days was back. Judy was back!

"If this isn't a miracle, what is?" Dr. Mugambi asked. "In all the years I've done surgery here, I have never felt so calm and assured about what I'm doing like I was this evening. It wasn't that I knew Judy would get well, but that I felt in my heart I was doing what God had asked me to do. Instead of the ETV, I have a shunt, which is a superior form of the shunts that have been applied on Judy before. This time, I actually felt as if the angels were right in this room with us." He drew a deep breath, then added, "I now know that Judy will be okay!"

We later prayed again, then the doctor left us in the hands of a nurse. Over the next twenty four hours, the nurse and the doctor watched over Judy, intent on ensuring everything went well. It was like that until two days later, when we left Mbale for Kenya, but this time instead of making our way to Nairobi, we went home, where our relatives had organized a major prayer event for Judy.

Pastor Isaac Maiyo, an ordained minister of more than thirty years, and at the time the Church Pastor of Kapkonjusmo Church, which is also my local church, was called to lead in those prayers and for the first time I saw what Jacob went through on the night he wrestled God, because from the moment the pastor started praying, there was no pleading, he told God things a mere mortal like me wouldn't have said.

Let me tell you what he said…

———

Before we get to that prayer session, I have to tell you that in every man's life, you will always feel it when a corner has been turned.

The day we left Uganda, after this third visit, I felt a strong sense of victory. If what we had faced was the equivalent of climbing Mount Everest, I was now sure we were finally at the peak.

We were looking down at the plains yonder and wondering how uncertain and dangerous and discouraging the climb had been. For me, this was over, but I wasn't reckless enough to announce that upon my arrival in Mosoriot. Instead, we got home in the evening and asked to be allowed to rest. Prayers, I said, should be conducted the next day as we had agreed. The elders obliged.

*

Back in Nairobi, at our Nairobi East Church, members of the church kept us in prayer and many visited our girls at home to be sure they were safe.

**

My colleagues at the Kenya Institute of Management were just as determined to keep my girls safe and well taken care of. They called us day and night to ask what was happening and whether we needed them to raise any more funds for us. So gracious were friends and relatives that one day, after Elder Sam Otieno and his wife had called to pray with us, the debt I owed the church, the institute and friends all over the country became too much to bear.

On that night I broke down and wept, because I realized that all of us were members of one race: the human race. In a world Judy had so carefully created with her illness, there was neither a Luo nor a Kikuyu; neither a Kalenjin nor a Luhya; neither an Adventist nor a Catholic; we were all one. God's children. In Judy's coma, that's the world she saw—a wonderful place where love was the cornerstone of our existence and people of all races and colors and tribes and religions came together to share our common heritage: humanity. So was the pain of getting into such an idealistic world worth the sorrow we had endured?

Before we answer that question, let us get home from Mbale and allow Pastor Maiyo to pray for Judy!

Thirteen

Maiyo's Confounding Prayer

The day broke in Mosoriot as usual and it wasn't long before we all started moving about in an effort to make the home welcoming for the guests Judy would have later in the day. Eunice's father, a man who believed in his God with every bone in his body, had taken a leading role in preparations for the day of prayer.

Today, our prayers, according to my father-in-law, would be geared toward seeking complete healing for Judy. He wanted to bring in Pastor Maiyo, a youthful minister who many folks in the District he served had come to love and admire as a straight shooter. One of the spiritual sons of the late Pastor Maiyo, who had served as the President of Western Kenya Field, the younger Maiyo grew up under the shadow of his spiritual father and had watched with admiration as the old man traversed vast territories on a bicycle to proclaim the message of a soon returning Christ.

Stout and tough like most Nandis, the young pastor was known to speak his mind freely and mean what he said. With his heavy set frame and piercing eyes, he held his congregants spellbound whenever he delivered his sermons, because people knew he talked straight from the heart. By calling him here today, my father-in-law wanted to hear what the pastor would say about Judy's troubles. What, in the pastor's opinion, was God trying to achieve by keeping a child in this state? That's what the Mzee wanted to know today.

Preparations ran right into 11:30 a.m., the time visitors started to trickle in. We had no idea how many folks to expect in the home because Mzee had made a general call. What later surprised us was that at the height of the session, we had enough guests to cover the entire perimeter of the home. Word had spread far and wide about Judy's condition, how Eunice and I had spent money, time, and whatever else there was to spend, to save the girl, but nothing seemed to have so far worked. By coming here this afternoon, they too, in their small way, wanted to be part of something they saw as larger than themselves. The healing of this child, when it came, had to be owned by the village just as much as the folks in Nairobi would own it. Judy was theirs; she was their daughter; she was the baby that was now uniting a village in prayer because only the God of her grandfathers could heal her.

As the guests continued to roll in, I thought about my life in this village many years ago. I saw friends with whom I grew up and many who were older or younger than me at that time. The journey of life had brought us to different destinations, where some of us were now educated and on an upward social and economic trajectory while others seem to have stagnated in both. It was disheartening to see many who had exhibited tremendous potential but never went to secondary school because their parents couldn't afford the fees or saw no wisdom in sending them to higher school. In their place, I now had different friends like Reuben Ndinya, George Wachiuri, Sam Otieno and others. And even the language of my church was now different, because at our Nairobi East Church the pastor preached in English. My life had changed in ways that only coming back home, like we had done this time, could open my eyes to. I was stunned and grateful to God for His mercies and leadership in my life.

But I was also aware that the Lord didn't call someone for no reason. There was a reason the Lord had targeted me to give me a competitive education, get me a family, and get me on a path to a successful career. He had a purpose for me that I had to fulfil or my call would amount to nothing. It was while thinking about my blessings that I thought about the call of Moses. Moses was an old man in the Median Desert at the time of his call. Out of the blue, the Lord confronted him with a burning bush that wasn't consumed and told him, "I am the God of your fathers Abraham, Isaac and Jacob. I have heard the cry of my people in Egypt. I have come to send you to Pharaoh so that you may tell him to let my people go!"

If you were Moses, what would you have done? But that may not be the right question to ask; the right question is: are you aware that in whatever station of life you are the Lord has called you to minister to His people? I've heard many folks say that: I'm not a pastor, or I'm just a businessman, or I've already given to the church so let the church take care of other matters. This is wrong. We all have to remain cognizant of the fact that each of us is called. No life on earth has dropped here by mistake; we all have a role to play in closing the history of this earth. And so I looked at my own circumstances and asked the Lord to reveal why He brought me here. Why was I born? And why has He been so kind to me?

The answer to my question wouldn't come, though, until later in the afternoon, when Pastor Isaac Maiyo started to preach. A man of many words, his sermonette was brisk, loaded and urgent. In the presence of the Obwathos and Pastor Korir, who Mzee Nyango had invited, he explained the narrative that through the ages has linked suffering to sin and to man's fall in the Garden of Eden, then he declared that pain and suffering would never end in this world; it would end in the world to come. So for us who are alive, there is no reason to weep and pray as if we don't expect suffering to afflict us; we are all members of a fallen human race and we all face the dire consequences of sin the same way, whether we are black, white or yellow, he said.

But it was his prayer that would later make me open my eyes even as he still prayed. The pastor had followed the story of Judy's illness and had come to the conclusion that this had taken too long. The name of the Lord was being dragged in the mud because of the prolonged illness, he felt. And so when he started praying, he didn't mince words. Pumping his fist in the air and sounding agitated but controlled, he asked God how long this would take? Why aren't you acting, he demanded of God. Then he declared, "Lord, you can't let Judy continue to suffer like this. If it is not your will that she lives, let her rest so that this matter may be over with!"

My eyes opened!

After his brave, stern words, he prayed for those gathered at the home, then said amen. Now, if you know anything about Christians, the period following prayer and that amen is normally one of silence. Not this time. This time Pastor Maiyo's amen was followed by excited talk. People were happy to hear the young pastor talk to God as to a friend, as to someone he could discuss options with. I guess they were also glad that the fiery trait that had characterized Nandi leadership, whether in church or in politics, was alive in the young leader. He had lost his mother at the tender age of eight, then had to live with his maternal uncle Hosea Barngetuny, but he later overcame such adversity and studied for a diploma in Ministry at Kamagambo, a Bachelors in Theology at Spicer College, in Poona, India; and even a Masters in Pastoral Ministry at Solusi College, in Zimbabwe. They saw in this pastor a reflection of his spiritual father, Pastor Jackson Maiyo; and a reflection of great leaders like Bishop Alexander Kipsang arap Muge; but more so a reflection of the great warrior Koitalel arap Samoei. Because of the many challenges the community faced, only leadership of that quality could work among the people.

For me, though, it was that sermonette that later woke me up to a reality I never considered possible—the reality that a mere mortal could talk to God as to a friend. Even more baffling was the possibility that man could get tough with the Creator when occasion called for it. Was God so great that He could act on man's instructions yet feel not belittled? Was He so mighty that He could never lose face even when a pastor appeared to talk on equal terms with Him? These questions rang in my mind and I decided that when I got to Nairobi I would have a different kind of talk with God. I wanted to ask

Him, in the same tone Pastor Maiyo had talked to Him, what He wanted me to do for Him. I wanted Him to tell me in no uncertain terms what my role in this world is and what He would one day hold me accountable for. I was ready to follow Him and do whatever He asked me to do.

————

Eunice was also delighted by the way people poured into our home from villages across the plains and hills to pray for Judy. She was particularly touched by the way her dad had supported us and took a leading role in organizing the prayers. Later, as the event concluded and we were given a chance to thank Judy's many guests, Eunice narrated a moving story about the tribulations we had so far endured. She concluded by saying that Judy's pain had done something in our life. It has made us become deeply prayerful people. She was right!

*

Later that cloudy afternoon, we were hurriedly dropped off at the Eldoret International Airport, where we caught a flight to Nairobi. As far as I was concerned, this was the end of our travails, because I was convinced that it was the Lord who had done the surgery on Judy in Mbale this time. But even if there was a recurrence of a blockage, this time I wouldn't worry and fret about things; I now knew that Judy was not mine, but my father's. My father in heaven. And can you imagine what irony that was: that Judy and Eunice and our daughters and I actually had the same father?

**

We got to Nairobi and made it home safely. When we got to our house in Donholm, the girls were delighted to see Judy. They took her in their arms and took turns kissing her, talking to her, singing to her and reminding her how much she was loved and missed. But it was Joan who did something we didn't expect. When she got Judy into her arms, rather than do what her sisters had done, she cried, then prayed softly. Looking back, it is clear to us that it was on that day that Judy's deep friendship with Joan started. The two sisters have a special bond others in the house are yet to share!

Later in the night, we all retired to bed and I thanked God for the way He had led in our lives. It was now clear to me that Judy was a miracle girl who had already touched so many people and brought them into her world where faith and prayer were the dandelions that kept the streets bright day and night.

***

Three months after Judy's last surgery, we went back to Mbale for a regular checkup. Let me tell you what happened…

Fourteen

Final Trip To Mbale

The day after we came back from Uganda, Eunice and I stayed home to observe Judy. We didn't want surprises even though we were pretty comfortable in the feeling that the Lord had finally stepped in to end Judy's incessant agony. After that first day, we watched Judy through the week, then through the month, then over the next month, and finally on the third month the day came to return her to Dr. Mugambi. This time our trip to Uganda wasn't going to be one of tears, but one of joy. It was the first time we were coming to Mbale with good news for the doctor, because even though there were minor issues with the functioning of the new shunt, which he had inserted to replace the two shunts, Judy's head hadn't grown any bigger. I was sure he too looked forward to the news of Judy's relatively stable life after what we were all sure was God's direct intervention in her life.

We left Nairobi on the morning flight to Eldoret, then linked up with Elkana. Our drive to Mbale, because we were in a taxi, didn't take long. In fact, we made it in time to catch up with Dr. Mugambi before he closed shop for the day. And what a wonderful reunion it was. The perpetually optimistic Ugandan doctor was so delighted to see Judy and was even more taken by the news that Judy's condition had remarkably improved. Taking Judy in his arms, he prayed for the girl and said, "The worst part is over, Judy!"

I knew he was right. Even Eunice and Elkana felt that indeed the worst part was over. The doctor went on to assess the shunt and looked closely at Judy's vitals. Other than minor functional issues, which he corrected without too much trouble, he was impressed by what he saw and declared Judy's progress acceptable. He hoped her recovery would continue down the same path. That night, as we drove back to Eldoret, I was reminded of the story of Job once again. Job, after he had endured his trials without any blemish, had his health restored and his wealth multiplied beyond measure. Was the Lord going to do the same for us? Had we passed the test?

I had no way of knowing whether we had or not, but I knew that I had one night confronted God the same way Pastor Maiyo had three months ago. I had promised Him that if He revealed to me why He placed me here, I would serve Him all the days of my life. It was on that night that the image of eternity flashed right before me. In that image, I saw God acting to save man from the snares of the devil. So surprised was I by the simplicity of salvation that I wondered why man had weaved such a complex narrative about it. What the Lord wanted each of us to do was to accept Him as the Creator of the universe and to worship Him for the great wonders He had performed in our lives. That was it. Making salvation follow patterns like big tithe, getting early to church and being a vegetarian were matters of consequence to our health and longevity in this world, but had nothing to do with our salvation—they were mere pointers to a healthy lifestyle.

"You are so quiet," Eunice finally said as we approached Eldoret International Airport. I could tell she had been sleeping and had just woken up. We dropped off Elkana at a corner stage, then proceeded to the airport. Our desire was to be in Nairobi by 9:00 p.m.

By God's grace, we made it home around 10:00 p.m. and worshipped as a family before the girls retired to bed. As for Eunice and I, we stayed up to thank God for His amazing grace that had saved our daughter from what seemed like inevitable death. We reminisced over the last couple of months and shook our heads in disbelief at how the Lord had acted powerfully to reveal Himself to us in ways no pastor could have ever done. We now knew the Lord in a way we never had before, because what we had before was faith based on the teachings of our fathers; but now we knew Him based on the teachings He Himself had placed in our hearts. The Lord who had healed Jairo's daughter and resurrected Lazarus on the third day was now our personal friend. I knew that going forward, our family would never be the same again. And even though we still had to see Dr. Mugambi in another three months, I no longer feared anything. Victory was ours in the Lord and Satan would never scare us again!

——

Six months after Judy's final surgery, we took her to Mbale again as the doctor had advised. This time, when we got there, we were more concerned about the eroding beauty of Mt. Elgon than Judy's illness. Our exuberance was affirmed when Dr. Mugambi swept into the room and didn't even bother to assess Judy the same way he had done three months ago. Like us, he was now persuaded that Judy's healing was not going to be stopped by anything. The miracle was complete!

*

A year later we took Judy back to Mbale to satisfy Dr. Mugambi's requirement for a visit at that time. When we got there, it was the first time our visit was more of a friendly nature than one of a patient-doctor type. We spent nearly an hour talking about the grim days when Judy first visited the hospital. But we dwelt more on the third visit, when we had come to the hospital with Judy in a coma.

"How did you get clearance at the airport with the girl in a coma?" the doctor asked, finally eager to find out how we had done something so daring.

Eunice said, "God blinded the officers at Immigration!"

Later we left Mbale and went back to Nairobi satisfied that Judy was now well. In spite of her paralyzed right side and the fact that she had to permanently have that shunt that drained water from her head, we knew that Judy would no longer have to face a dark night like she had faced since being born. What we now had to worry about was what school Judy would go to and the amount of supervision she would need at home, at church, at school and on the playground. Judy's dark night had turned to day and her world would be bright from now on, because God's surgery would never be reversed.

Fifteen

Judy's Amazing World

It has now been five years since Judy was last seen by any doctor regarding her condition. The last one was nearly four years ago when we took her to Mbale. In the four years we have been with Judy, the jovial, playful girl has welcomed us into her amazing world and we have been tremendously blessed by her kindness, loving nature and openness. As we talk about her world, we must begin by telling you that her favorite song is…take a guess? It is *Burdens Are Lifted At Calvary*. This is the song that when she starts singing you'll find yourself moved to tears because it is as if she understands that her safety lies in her bed being made at the foot of the cross.

In our Nairobi East Church, Sister Millicent Okeyo has made it a point to always pick Judy and take her to the front to sing whenever children sing. At her age, our daughter understands what it means to be in church and what Christ means to us. When the pastor or anybody else prays, she shuts her eyes and clasps her hands in reverence to God. And when asked to pray, she talks to God as to a dear friend. Her sense of right and wrong is acute because we have trained her to understand evil and good. Her Sabbath school teachers and her classmates treat her just like they treat everyone else. If there is one thing I thank God for, it is that Judy knows and loves Him. And though she calls me Daddy, she knows that there is another father far greater than me. Her father in heaven!

But it is not only her spiritual life that defines who she is. Judy has also been keen on school, as exhibited by her sitting at "class" with her sisters when they are tutored by Teacher Hellen. In moments of "class," Judy sits calmly near the teacher and writes her ABCD... She can count up to 30 and takes great pride in her ability to go toe-to-toe with her sisters, who she sees as older than her and she respects and loves.

We have come to the point where we now believe that the better course of action for Judy would be to take her to a formal school. We don't want her to feel any less than children her age, even though she will have to begin school much later than they did.

Eunice and I have voted to take her to Good Testimony Primary School, right there where we live at Nyayo Embakasi, because we believe she will be taken better care of within that system and she will flourish there. When we ask her what she wants to be, she says Doctor. I believe the Lord who has healed her and brought her this far will take her as far as her heart desires. Yes, Judy will one day be a doctor, because the love she has for people cannot stay trapped within her body; it will have to manifest itself in the way she tearfully touches the burdens of others afflicted like her.

And when Judy becomes a doctor, there will be only one person to thank for the turn of events in her life, other than God. It is her sister Janet. Now a student at Bishop Gatimu Ngandu Girls High School, in Nyeri, it was Janet who wrote a heartfelt letter when she learnt that Eunice and I had decided to take Judy to a school for the disabled in Naromoru. Before she left for school one morning, she tucked the letter under our blanket and never told anybody about it. Later, when her mom and I came to sleep, we got the letter. Read for yourself:

To Baba,

I don't think taking Judy to boarding (Naromoru Disabled Children's Home) will be good.

I just don't want you to regret your decision and I want Judy to grow up in a motherly and fatherly environment. Many girls and boys have passed through bad things. I mean that when you leave your child under the care of people you don't know about their character, then they, she or he will likely copy their character.

Baba I am not saying this to discourage but to enlighten you. I was looking for enough time but could not find it. Hope you may understand me. We will talk more when you come back from home. SAFE JOURNEY.

From Janet

August 27, 2013

Eunice and I were deeply touched and we changed our minds about Naromoru; Judy would go to a different school!

But it is in the area of her health that we still face some challenges. Not too long ago, my friend Reuben Ndinya visited from South Africa and asked why I hadn't taken Judy to India for treatment. His question caught me off-guard because I hadn't considered it urgent to take Judy to India to have doctors there look into matters of her paralyzed right side. Whatever caused that paralysis, the girl remains unable to move her right limbs and cannot write with her right hand either.

In the coming days, Eunice and I plan to take Judy to India, where we have been told by friends that at the Apollo Hospital, in Hyderabad, in the state of Uttar Pradesh, there are doctors who can help Judy regain use of her right leg and hand. As much as we can't predict what will happen when we do so, we owe it to her to try everything under our power. I want to be able to look my daughter in the eye someday and tell her, "Sweetheart, Dad and Mom tried everything!"

Back at home, Judy's sisters, her mom and I have probably been the ones who have enjoyed some of the most intimate moments with Judy. We have watched her grow from her tender age to who she is today. We have seen her smile, laugh, cry and even scold. She wears the brightest smile when she sees us after a while and loves to sit with us to recount events of her day. At night, she chooses who she will sleep with, depending on her mood. When she's happy, she sleeps with Joan, when she is sick she sleeps with Mama and I, but when Janet comes back from school, she gives her one night to tell her stories.

She loves playing Hide and Seek with her sisters and laughs heartily when either Joan or Dorothy, who is now a student at Precious Blood Kilunguni, in Makueni County, find her. It is in moments like those that the amazing Judy blossoms into a flower that lights up the neighborhood with cheer and fragile innocence. And though many times she wants to follow her friends on the streets to ride her bike—her green bike—we are always weary of something going wrong, so we keep a protective eye from a distance. I know she doesn't mind our presence because we always sense her desire that one of us be around as she plays. The reassurance she gets from our being around helps her enjoy playing without fear of harm from anyone or anything.

About two years or so ago, the Lord has done amazing things in our life. Eunice has finally gotten a job as a Research Officer at the National Cereals and Produce Board; and I have been promoted from Deputy CEO and Director of Strategy at the Kenya Institute of Management to the Acting Vice Chancellor of the Management University of Africa. In my wildest dreams, I never knew I could have come this far, but the Lord has led the way. I'm only bringing this up to tell you how Judy prays for us whenever we're about to leave for work. She always says: Dear Lord, help Daddy and Mommy as they go out to get me *unga* (flour!). And later in the evening, when we get back, she stands by the door and welcomes each of us with the brightest of smiles.

In the five years we have been with Judy, we have learnt a lot about her, about her heavenly father and about our friends. But the time has now come to share our miracle girl with the rest of the world. She will begin her long journey at Good Testimony Primary School, then she will go on to brighten a world that doesn't have as many angels as it should have, because if she ever fails to hold a stethoscope to heal a child with arrhythmia or meningitis or problematic conjunctivitis, she will surely heal someone with loneliness by showering upon them the smile of an angel.

We remain indebted to so many friends who have played a number of roles in Judy's life. We can't thank enough my former boss and current CEO of K.I.M. Dr. David Muturi, who encouraged us and asked about Judy daily; our brothers Mark Nyango and Enos Letting, for donating blood for their niece after her surgery at Mater; Elder Sam and Jennifer Otieno, who have walked with us since the early days of Judy's life and are today helping her with a treatment known as hydrotherapy.

Dr. Bernadette Mungai and Barrack Muluka, who kept reassuring us that all would be well; the elders at Nairobi East, who have availed themselves to pray with us whenever we needed encouragement; Pastors Timothy Guto of Nairobi East and Isaac Maiyo, who have pleaded with God to heal the little girl; the women of Nairobi East church, who have prayed and kept Eunice company in her lowest moments; the doctors at Mater, Nairobi Hospital, Gertrude's and Kijabe, who took time to help Judy heal; Rueben Ndinya and Sarah Serem, for leading in the fundraising effort. But we, as a family, want to especially thank Dr. Mugambi and the team at CURE International, in Mbale, for letting God use him to finally get Judy on a path to healing.

Of course Anne Ngugi; and Pastor Sylas Tochim, of Birmingham University, holds a dear place in our hearts for being there for us at critical moments.

The journey ahead remains long and may prove dreary at times, but this is a burden we left at the cross four years ago, so we no longer feel the weight of anything. In any case, the Lord has surrounded us with such great friends, a great church and great children. We go forward in the firm belief that Judy's world is a place of refuge and strength, where those who enter cannot leave without meeting the Creator of the universe, because in that world, the smile of a little angel reveals the face of a Savior who died on the cross for all our sins.

I know you are secretly wondering whether we expect Judy to completely heal and one day run for Kenya at the Olympics. Let me tell you what our hope for Judy is in the epilogue.

Epilogue

Many years ago, a Russian cosmonaut called Yuri Gagarin shot into space and circled the universe at supersonic speed. Expected by his expectant team at the Russian Federal Space Agency to gather every last relevant detail for analysis when he got back to earth, he did the best he could to leave such a firm thumbprint on space exploration that future Russians would be proud of. But more than anything else, he worked hard to set Russia on a path to dominance in space wars, where he was sure it wouldn't be long before the Americans and future emergent world powers tried to stamp their authority as well. He did what he could and Russians christened him a hero for his amazing efforts.

When Yuri came back to earth, he was asked by excited folks what he had seen in space. True to his background as a nonbeliever, the boastful cosmonaut declared that he went all over the place and saw everything there was to see, but he didn't see God.

As far as he was concerned, God was a figment of man's fertile imagination. He was one among those folks who believed that man invented God because a being such as God was needed to answer man's most vexing questions.

Years later another astronaut went to space. This time it was an American called John Glenn. John went into space and was immediately confounded by the majesty of what he saw. As his spacecraft shot through space and he saw planet earth from out there, he declared, like the Psalmist once did, that the heavens declare the glory of God. So moved was John that when he was asked what he had seen out there, he knelt in reverence to the God who created the amazing wonders he had seen. He was humbled that such a God would ever worry about him, a son of mere mortals in Ohio.

Like Yuri, Americans showered praise on John, and the folks in Ohio even elected him a senator, but he never, for a moment, forgot what he saw in space, because Senator John Glenn had something Yuri Gagarin didn't have. He had eyes that saw what the Lord wanted him to see!

As our girl Judy grows up in this blind, deaf world, Eunice and I have only one desire for her—that she will grow up under the protective wing of her father in heaven. We pray that whoever interacts with her will come away touched by her kindness and will see Christ in her. If like John Glenn she can see the world through the inner eyes of faith, that is all Eunice and I can ever ask for, because that will mean she has transformed her life of burden into a world of joy. So let me directly answer the question on your mind about our expectations for Judy. We expect that she will go to Good Testimony Primary School, then to secondary school and eventually to college. That's all we can say for now. We want to take it one day at a time.

We have shared Judy with you—and are now sharing her with the world. Whenever and wherever you meet Judy and other children like her, stop and say hello. She may smile, look away or even look at you with stern eyes, but don't think it is because she doesn't like you; it is because in her world honesty is the leading virtue. Judy loves each of you and thanks you for sharing her amazing life of miracles and victories won through tears and fervent prayer. We remain hopeful that a permanent cure will be found for congenital hydrocephalous and all the other maladies that afflict little children.

May the God of Senator John Glenn be the God of Judy all the days of her life. We leave you with Judy's favorite song in the next page.

You may sing with her…

Burdens Are Lifted At Calvary

Days are filled with sorrow and care,
Hearts are lonely and drear;
Burdens are lifted at Calvary,
Jesus is very near.

Refrain

Burdens are lifted at Calvary,
Calvary, Calvary,
Burdens are lifted at Calvary,
Jesus is very near.

Cast your care on Jesus today,
Leave your worry and fear;
Burdens are lifted at Calvary,
Jesus is very near.

Troubled soul, the Saviour can see,
Ev'ry heartache and tear;
Burdens are lifted at Calvary
Jesus is very near.

Judy

Judy enjoying a piggy back ride with her sister Joan

Mom, Judy, and Dad
as Judy celebrated her
5th birthday

Judy in the company of Daddy, Joan(left), and Joyce (right)

Judy's tenderly held in the arms of her best friend, Millicent Okeyo

The Lettings

Other Great Books By Sahel Publishing Association

There will be many more books that will answer life's toughest questions for you, because as we always say, Sahel Publishing Association's promise is: Books that Speak To Your Hopes and Fears. Call us today: **0715.596.106 or 0731.651.927**. Talk to one of Africa's most-sought ghostwriters and editors, Hon Sam Okello, about your writing dreams!

Visit any of our authors at: www.amazon.com

Our website: www.sahelpublishing.net

We are in Kenya, the U.S.A., The U.K. and India

Publish your book with us today!

Disclaimer

Some of the information used in this narrative has been sourced from the Internet. We have also used information from *Wikipedia*, the Mater Hospital website, Gertrude's Children's Hospital website, Kijabe Mission Hospital website and CURE International website. The information has only been used to establish a background for the narrative.